CATC

Welcome to
The iPhone Book™

The iPhone has swiftly become one of the most groundbreaking and innovative devices available on the market. It has taken the humble phone and made it an all-encompassing multimedia device that can be used in every area of your life. With the latest updates in iOS 5, it has become even more useful, with functions like Siri's voice control, Safari Reader and iCloud extending its already fantastic functionality. With so much that this little smartphone can do, the second volume of The iPhone Book has been revised to include the latest from iCloud and the iPhone 4S to show you how to get the very best out of your device. From understanding the core apps in our Getting Started section, to the best productivity, lifestyle and entertainment apps you can find, The iPhone Book will help you to master your smartphone in no time at all. We hope you enjoy the book.

The iPhone Book

Imagine Publishing Ltd
Richmond House
33 Richmond Hill
Bournemouth
Dorset BH2 6EZ
☎ +44 (0) 1202 586200
Website: www.imagine-publishing.co.uk
Twitter: @Books_Imagine
Facebook: www.facebook.com/ImagineBookazines

Editor in Chief
Dave Harfield

Production Editor
Sarah Harrison

Senior Art Editor
Danielle Dixon

Design
Charlie Crooks

Printed by
William Gibbons, 26 Planetary Road, Willenhall, West Midlands, WV13 3XT

Distributed in the UK & Eire by
Imagine Publishing Ltd, www.imagineshop.co.uk. Tel 01202 586200

Distributed in Australia by
Gordon & Gotch, Equinox Centre, 18 Rodborough Road, Frenchs Forest,
NSW 2086. Tel + 61 2 9972 8800

Distributed in the Rest of the World by
Marketforce, Blue Fin Building, 110 Southwark Street, London, SE1 0SU.

Part of the

bookazine series

IMAGINE PUBLISHING

The iPhone Book
Contents

Page 8:
Ultimate guide to the iPhone
Get the most out of your device

 Essential apps

"With iOS 5 your
iPhone is now
the ultimate
mobile device"

 Entertainment

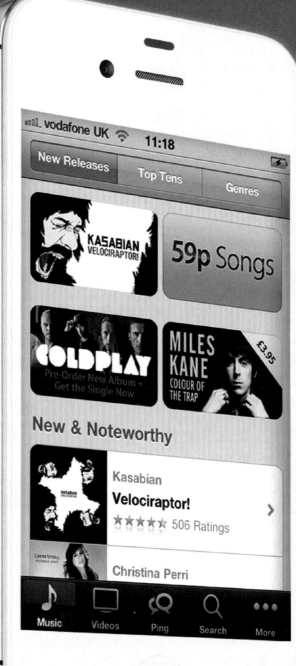

Ultimate
guide to the
iPhone

From downloading magazines to using voice control, the iPhone can help you work, rest and play

The iPhone is more than just a phone. It will help you achieve what you need to, it will help you communicate with friends, and it will help you to have fun. It can undertake thousands of different tasks thanks to a large library of good quality apps and can also serve as the hub for your entertainment needs, be they music, video or photography.

The launch of iOS 5 has further enhanced the flexibility and potential functionality of the iPhone by including full integration with Twitter, a much improved notification system and more subtle improvements which come together to create a mobile environment that lets you get on with your life. There are many new tweaks to the core software and wider ranging changes which are more obvious, but the major benefit is speed and efficiency.

Everything you need to do on the iPhone is now visibly a little sharper, and time-wise a little snappier and at no point should you notice any slow-downs in action. The iOS package is comprehensive and it is now a mobile operating system that can help you in all parts of your life. Whatever you want to do with your phone, you can do it on an iPhone and here we will explain why.

Lifestyle

There's an app for
every single part
of your life

A smartphone is supposed to fit into your life and if it is clever enough, it can greatly enhance how you manage your communications with friends and also your free time. When you consider what an iPhone is capable of, there really are few areas that it cannot cope with. Social networking is covered by the full integration of Twitter into the operating system and the Facebook app works just as well as the main desktop site. Google+, Instagram and all of the other major social networks are catered for so you can be sharing photos, videos and your thoughts 24 hours a day if you like.

The photographic capabilities of all iPhones are also impressive and there is no excuse for letting special moments pass you by. You can

edit your photos and share them with the world in seconds and potentially even upload them to your own blog. The cameras on the latest iPhones can snap photos that some compact cameras can only dream of and the ability to create a home movie on just the phone takes creation to a whole new level.

Blogs and websites can be managed using just an iPhone thanks to the advanced web browser and a variety of apps designed for specific services, and you can also hold group chats with friends or hold a video chat over

"You can edit your photos and share them in seconds"

FaceTime. If you are away on business and want to talk to your children, simply find a Wi-Fi hotspot and spend a few minutes speaking face to face with those who are the most important to you. It is all too easy to keep in contact with people using whatever method you like and potentially your lifestyle will be greatly enhanced by the communication features built in to every iPhone. iMessage lets you send instant messages to your friends for free and the clean and simple interface used within messaging ensures that the conversation will keep flowing.

Potentially an iPhone can do almost everything a desktop PC can, but with the advantage of always being with you. Whether you want to call a friend while you are waiting

Top ways to improve your everyday life
Enhance your lifestyle with iOS 5

01 You can now Tweet from anywhere
Twitter has been integrated widely within iOS 5 and now lets you use the service in every core app. For example, you can send a tweet with a photo direct from the photos app which only requires a couple of taps. You can send webpage links to Twitter via the web menu and you can even tweet locations from the Maps app. It is an incredibly subtle implementation, but one that works perfectly.

02 Tweak your photos to perfection
An iPhone is capable of taking fantastic quality photos, but some will still require touching up to make them look exactly as you would like. You can now view any saved photo and crop it, auto-enhance it or remove red-eye in a matter of seconds. More advanced editing features are available in third party apps, but the changes you need to make most often are now built in to iOS 5.

03 Quicker photos
Photography is all about capturing the moment and the iPhone is now the ideal tool for this thanks to the updates in iOS 5. Double-tap the home button when on the lock screen, to see a camera icon pop up. Tap it and you can take a photo immediately. This means that you are more likely to capture the shot before it has passed, meaning you'll never miss that one-time-only moment ever again.

04 Free text messages
iMessage is possibly the most subtle of all the new iOS 5 features, but one which could save you a lot of money. It sits in the standard messaging app and will automatically send an iMessage in place of a text message if the recipient is also using an iOS 5 enabled iPhone. The only change you will see is that the messages are blue instead of green, and that of course they are free.

05 Wireless syncing
The ability to wirelessly synchronise with iTunes can make a big difference to the way you use your iPhone because you are no longer tied to a physical PC. This will save you time and likely make you synchronise more often which in turn will ensure that your backed up data is more secure and more recent. It is a feature that should arguably have been implemented a long time ago, but it has finally arrived to make your life a little easier.

for a bus or simply update your Twitter feed, it can be done and usually without needing to think about what you are doing. The iPhone is designed to fit into your life, no matter how busy it is, and over time you'll find that the features and tasks you undertake come naturally. The battery is capable of powering through the most intense of days and the voice quality ensures that you'll be heard. It is designed to let you share your life with others and to get a glimpse of how they spend their days, and there are few alternatives that even come close to the iPhone experience. Some things in life are priceless and keeping in touch with those you love definitely falls into this category.

Productivity

Make your daily tasks much easier with the iPhone's extensive functionality

With so many computerised aids available today it is easy to get stuck in a tangled web of emails, messages and distractions that reduce your productivity. The iPhone, on the other hand, can be the best assistant you can have to help you fulfil your to do list. Siri is an example of a technology that will speed up many of your daily tasks; you can 'speak' emails, texts and memos and gather information without ever touching your phone and with practice your smartphone usage will change completely. You can create Office documents and email

them directly from an iPhone and also initiate conference calls at short notice with just a few taps. Your Calendar is always on hand to manage your schedule and Reminders will alert you to time-specific tasks that need completing. It all works together and at times the various apps and features will interact with each other to create solutions that keep the stress away and your productivity levels high.

You can respond in an instant and share information no matter what your location, but at times the less obvious solutions help you more. Deadly accurate navigation apps will

help you get to meetings on time and avoid traffic every day. If you live in an area with constant traffic problems, this could save you an hour every day. Meeting minutes can be typed up on the move or you can record the entire meeting for referring to in the future. When you consider these features alongside the contacts, calendar, tasks, emailing and everything else that can be undertaken on an iPhone it really does become the ideal assistant for your busiest of days.

Constant interruptions are the plague of modern living thanks to the various ways that people can contact you, but the notifications within iOS ensure that you are not interrupted when you are busy. They sit in the background and only need to be seen when you want to view them. A constant stream of information is also being pushed to your phone in real-time. Stock prices, the weather, important news and other

Be more productive

Top iPhone tips to help you with your daily tasks

03 Remember everything

The new Reminders app in iOS 5 is incredibly basic and at first glance looks as though it cannot compete with the more advanced alternatives available in the App Store. It does, however, work seamlessly with Siri and over time the simple interface actually becomes an advantage. You will never forget anything again if you use it wisely and it highlights that the simplest solutions often work better for day-to-day tasks.

"You can also manage many mailboxes"

01 The best personal assistant ever

Siri is not like virtual assistants of the past because it bears all of the Apple hallmarks in terms of usability and quality. You can speak naturally into your iPhone and gain answers to difficult questions, set alarms and use it to write emails and texts. It is the kind of system that grabs you and in a matter of days you will forget what it felt like to type on your iPhone.

02 Proper notifications

Previously, notifications on an iPhone were intrusive, clumsy and often very annoying. Thankfully, they now work as they should and appear briefly before disappearing into the background. When you want to check your notifications you simply need to slide down the top bar to see what you have missed. It couldn't be simpler. The fact that you can customise each type of notification is a brilliant added bonus.

04 Communicating

Email is still the default method of communicating for most people and the iPhone implementation squeezes in all of the main features you will need within an interface that is exceptionally easy to use. Emails can be printed wirelessly, moved to specific folders in your email account and you can also manage as many mailboxes as you like in the one screen. It is still one of the best mobile communication solutions in the world.

events can affect your working day, but again the iPhone will either deliver them directly to you or wait until you are ready. It is designed to work in conjunction with your needs and not to dictate what you do.

Even the most advanced tasks are covered such as desktop publishing and image creation. There are countless examples of talented people creating realistic works of art on an iPhone and more creative methods of using an iPhone are being made available every day. You would be hard pushed to find a task the iPhone cannot cope with. It sounds too good to be true, but it is a fact that for creating things and making the most of your days, an iPhone is able to help you every step of the way.

"The iPhone is designed to work with your needs"

05 In the Cloud

iCloud is one of the biggest new features available to iPhone users and a place which lets you store all of your most important information for when you need it. This gives you access to all of your content and it will be pushed to every iOS device you own in real-time. Everything from your music and videos to emails and contacts will be safely backed up and available whenever you need them.

Entertainment

Your iPhone isn't just for making calls. We show you how to get more from the ultimate multimedia device

There are obvious limitations to entertainment on any smartphone with the screen size being the main obstacle. This would normally inhibit the ability to read eBooks, play games and watch videos, but strangely this limitation is unnoticeable once you have used an iPhone for a few days. The operating system and most apps have been designed with care to make the most of the limited space and this ultimately brings an experience that offers the perfect balance for such a pocketable device.

iPhone gaming has received lots of publicity and with good reason. The big name developers have jumped on board and are now producing titles that compete well with the best console titles. The success of *Angry Birds* is the perfect example of how big this market is and it is set to get bigger and offer even more choice in the future. Music is catered for by hardware that is capable of producing clear audio and the iTunes ecosystem lets you purchase music in an instant and then back it up to iCloud. You

can also rent and buy movies from iTunes for watching on your phone, or even purchase a cheap cable to play the films on your TV.

Every media format is available on the iPhone; books, movies, TV series, music, games, magazines, podcasts and more are just a few taps away and in no time your iPhone could become your media hub. Besides playing your films through a TV, you can play your music wirelessly through a car stereo or simply share your home videos with friends using the above average iPhone speaker.

The iPhone brand has reached a level that pushes content publishers to develop for it and to offer their media to its users. Amazon offers eBooks and DRM-free music for iOS and other services also support the iPhone so you can also spend time shopping around to get the best price. This means that your choices are almost limitless and this alone may stop you considering alternative platforms for your entertainment needs. It is a one-stop shop that will also present the news to you via the enhanced internet browser, the latest events

via news feeds and photos shared by friends over social networks.

Entertainment is usually enjoyed most with friends and multi-player gaming is fully supported in many apps. Whether you want to play against friends in the same room over Wi-Fi or against a group of strangers from around the world, you can do so thanks to some clever programming from app developers and Apple. You can play a simple word game and await the next move from your opponent on the other side of the world or join in a first-person battle against the enemy in realistic environments.

The iPhone can in theory fill up your whole day with different types of entertainment and this is potentially the only downside. It is, at times, very difficult to put down!

"Every media format is available on the iPhone"

Have fun with your iPhone

Your entertainment needs are easily met

01 Mobile magazines

Magazines have gradually made the move to mobile devices and the arrival of Newsstand in the iTunes Store is a major boon for the format. The Newsstand app collects all of your magazines under one icon and lets you purchase single issues or subscribe for longer periods if you want. The major publishers have all signed up to the format and it is already proving to be a big success. It is a simple idea that works very well.

02 Gaming

Gaming on an iPhone is a wonderful experience, and one that is enhanced by Game Center. It lets you compete against friends in any game you both play and also monitors your high scores in every game you play. Sometimes beating your personal best is all the encouragement you need to play 'just one more time' and the added element of competition against those closest to you makes it a valuable addition to any iPhone.

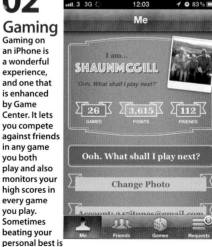

"The iPhone brand pushes publishers to offer more"

03
Web
The internet can be a source of entertainment as well as information and the browser in iOS 5 is now quicker than ever. It also manages to make even the most complicated sites easy to read on the iPhone screen, especially with Reader, which strips back all but the most important information. Providing a site is not Flash based, you can entertain yourself for hours using the internet on an iPhone.

04
eBooks
eBooks are quickly catching up with traditional books for market share and the iPhone is not lacking in options. iBooks is the default offering from Apple which lets you synchronise your reading position over multiple iOS devices and the Kindle offering from Amazon is just as impressive. You now have millions of eBooks at your disposal to read wherever and whenever you like, and often they are cheaper than their paper counterparts.

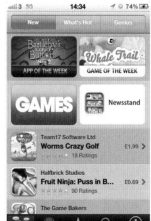

05
Apps
There are thousands of apps and games available for your iPhone and some stretch the boundaries of what we thought possible only a year ago. From complex gaming to sophisticated solutions, you'll find apps that can cope with many tasks. Its even better when the majority only cost a few pennies.

Top iPhone tips for…

The office

Work with greater speed and efficiency with these useful tips

Your iPhone is the ideal tool to help speed up your daily workflow, both in and out of the office. It's a tiny computer you can carry around in your pocket, updating documents and spreadsheets, sending emails quickly while commuting, and staying up to date with your co-workers through chat applications like FaceTime and Skype. Still, there are a few things that you can do to boost your productivity even more…

01
Set up iCloud

As we've said, iCloud is a brilliant new service from Apple that allows you to keep everything in sync across your devices, and backed up in case you ever lose your data. To switch it on, head into Settings and choose iCloud, then log in with your Apple ID. You can then select what you want to sync, including contacts and documents, so switch these on to ensure your data is completely safe and available online even if you don't have your iPhone with you.

Difficulty rating: Expert

Time taken: 15 minutes

"Update documents and spreadsheets"

02
Custom vibrations

A great way of knowing who is calling you before you look at your screen is using custom vibrations. You can create new vibration patterns through the contact you want to assign it to. Open up Contacts and find a colleague. Edit their card, tap on Vibration and hit Create New Vibration. Then you can tap out a pattern for the vibration, and when you feel this pattern you'll know who is calling or texting you.

Difficulty rating: Intermediate

Time taken: 5 minutes

03
Keyboard shortcuts

In the Settings app you can edit keyboards. Tap General, then Keyboard and scroll to the bottom of the page. You can then tap Add New Shortcut to create a quick way of typing to speed things up. For example, you can type 'omw' into one box, and 'on my way' into the other, and from then on every time you input those three letters it will expand into the words – perfect for speeding up the typing process.

Difficulty rating: Beginner

Time taken: 5 minutes

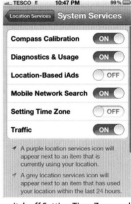

04
Prolong battery

There are plenty of tips on saving battery life, but one of the best is switching off some location services, as they drain it rapidly. Go to settings> Location Services and scroll down to the bottom. In System Services, switch off Setting Time Zone and Location-Based iAds. The former changes the timezone automatically but, unless you travel frequently, this is redundant, and as it regularly uses your data connection to scan for any changes, this will save battery power too.

Difficulty rating: Intermediate

Time taken: 2 minutes

05
Edit your signature

When you send an email from your iPhone, an automatic signature says 'Sent from my iPhone'. If you want to change this, go to Settings. Scroll down and select Mail, Contacts and Calendars. Next, tap on the Signature button under the Mail heading and you'll see a dialog box to enter text into. Add your signature and press Save for it to be added to future emails.

Difficulty rating: Beginner

Time taken: 5 minutes

Top iPhone tips for…
Organisation

Keep on top of your schedule with these essential hints

Your iPhone is well equipped to get you organised thanks to the quantity of useful data it can hold. Contacts, emails, photos and documents can all be stored, and with everything in one device – and that device being portable – it's the perfect pocket-sized PA. If you're already well organised, we've come up with ideas for how to get your phone, and your life, even more in order.

01 Delete apps fast

While it's common knowledge that you can delete apps by holding down a finger on one and tapping the 'X' in the corner, there's a much quicker way to erase them if you want to get rid of a lot in one go. Head into Settings, then into General and tap Usage. Every app that you have installed will be listed here, and if you tap one you can delete it instantly.

Difficulty rating: Beginner

Time taken: 3 minutes

02 Streamlining search

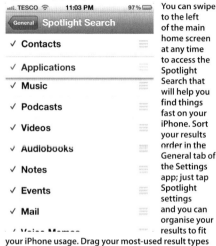

You can swipe to the left of the main home screen at any time to access the Spotlight Search that will help you find things fast on your iPhone. Sort your results order in the General tab of the Settings app; just tap Spotlight settings and you can organise your results to fit your iPhone usage. Drag your most-used result types to the top and uncheck those you don't want to trim down your search results.

Difficulty rating: Beginner

Time taken: 5 minutes

03 Battery accuracy

The iPhone normally displays a battery meter in the top-right corner, however it's not exactly the most accurate reading. If you want to see a percentage of the remaining battery, open Settings and hit General. Next, tap Usage and switch the Battery Percentage button to On. This will give you a better idea of how much power you have left to time your next top-up to perfection.

Difficulty rating: Beginner

Time taken: 1 minute

04 Sort notifications

The Notifications Center in iOS 5 makes sorting out all of your notifications super-easy. Swipe down from the top of the screen and you can see all your latest updates from various apps. However, you can sort out the order of these so those you value more are at the top of the menu by heading into Settings>Notifications. Tap Edit in the corner and drag them into the best sequence for you.

Difficulty rating: Beginner

Time taken: 3 minutes

05 Clean up your home screen

Deleting apps might be as easy as holding your finger on them and tapping the 'X', but the apps that come pre-installed on your device are harder to remove. However, if you don't use some of them and they're cluttering up your pages, head into Settings> General>Restrictions and type in your passcode. You can then switch off apps like iTunes that you don't want to see. When you return to the home screen you'll have a lot more space.

Difficulty rating: Intermediate

Time taken: 5 minutes

> "The quantity of useful data your iPhone can hold makes it the perfect pocket-sized PA"

Top iPhone tips for…
Photography
Ideas for getting the best out of your iPhone's powerful camera

The iPhone is more than just a phone, and one of its most brilliant features is its camera. Thanks to the new features of iOS 5, along with the incredible shooting system in the iPhone 4S, the camera is now not only truly powerful, but it offers a whole selection of features not available on normal cameras. Editing and sharing are both possible with your device, and here are our tips for getting the most out of both the hardware and software.

01 Save memory
The iPhone's HDR mode allows you to take fantastic photos, combining two shots: one with a high exposure and one with a low exposure. You can enable this in the Options menu of the camera, but by default your iPhone saves both the standard shot and the HDR shot. If you want to turn this off to save memory, go to Settings>Photos and scroll down to deactivate it.

Difficulty rating: Intermediate

Time taken: 2 minutes

02 Swipe to Album
When taking a snap, accessing the rest of your photos isn't as hard as you might think. While the small icon in the bottom-left does let you open your latest pics, this isn't the only way to get to your Camera Roll. Swipe in from the left of the screen and the camera interface will slide off, bringing up your most recent snaps.

Difficulty rating: Beginner

Time taken: 1 minute

"A whole selection of features not available on normal cameras"

03 Remote shutter
With iOS 5 comes the ability to capture shots with the Volume button, making photo-taking a whole lot easier. However, it's also possible to take snaps using a remote on a pair of headphones, giving you a way to shoot without needing to be holding your iPhone. This is perfect for taking group shots and also a really cool little tip for showing off to your friends.

Difficulty rating: Beginner

Time taken: 2 minutes

04 Autofocus lock
When taking a picture you can always tap on a part of the screen to focus your shot. However, it's less well known that you can lock the focus and exposure in one place too. All you need to do is hold your finger on the point in the photo you want to focus on and wait for the small AE/AF Lock icon to appear at the bottom of the screen.

Difficulty rating: Beginner

Time taken: 1 minute

05 Create new albums
Before iOS 5, the only way to create a new album of photos on your phone was to connect it up to your Mac or PC, open up iTunes and sync them across. Now, though, you can create new albums on your phone. First, head into the Camera Roll and tap the button in the top-right. Then, select some photos you want to place in your new album, tap Add to at the bottom, and choose New Album.

Difficulty rating: Intermediate

Time taken: 5 minutes

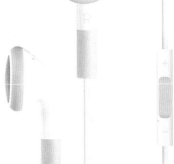

Top iPhone tips for…

Exercising
Allow your device to help you get fit

While some people might prefer a smaller device when they are exercising, the iPhone is a great item to take with you when you go for a run. Not only are there all kinds of apps to help you work out and get fit, but there is also a number of useful things that you can do to make your phone the perfect personal trainer.

01 Use VoiceOver

When working out you don't really have time to pull out your phone and start flicking through albums to find what you want to play, or your contacts to make a call. Thankfully, using Siri on a 4S, or VoiceOver on older iPhones, you can do it vocally. All you need to do is hold down the Pause button on your headphone controls and say a command.

Difficulty rating: Beginner

Time taken: 1 minute

02 Accessorise

While an iPhone is a great tool for helping you to exercise, if you invest in a few extras you can really make it a powerful implement. Accessories like a Nike+ Sensor or Bluetooth sports watch can keep track of your run as well as your heart rate, and if you don't like your phone being shaken around in your pocket you can get an armband to keep it more secure.

Difficulty rating: Beginner

Time taken: N/A

"The iPhone is a great item to take when you go for a run"

03 Switch on Nike + iPod

The iPhone actually contains an app made by sports giant Nike called Nike + iPod. To enable it, head into Settings and scroll to the bottom of the list. Tap the Nike + iPod menu icon and you can then flick the switch to the On position. You can now set up things like a PowerSong to get you through the hardest workouts, as well as keep track of runs if you own the Nike+ accessory.

Difficulty rating: Beginner

Time taken: 2 minutes

04 Use Genius

One of the most important things when you're out exercising is your music choice. You need something high-tempo and inspirational, and making a full playlist can take quite a while. If you want to make one much faster, pick one of your favourite songs for when you're working out and tap the Genius button on the Now Playing screen. You will now be delivered a playlist full of similar songs in just a couple of seconds.

Difficulty rating: Beginner

Time taken: 2 minutes

05 Turn off Shake to Shuffle

If you're out running or cycling, etc, you don't really want your music to keep skipping through tracks every time you take a step. The iPhone's Music app includes a Shake to Shuffle setting, which will skip to a random song if you shake the phone. To turn it on or off, head into Settings, then Music and slide the switch across. Now you can run along without any problems with jumping tunes.

Difficulty rating: Beginner

Time taken: 2 minutes

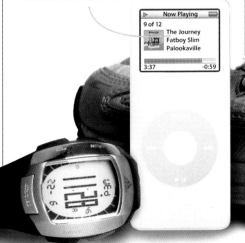

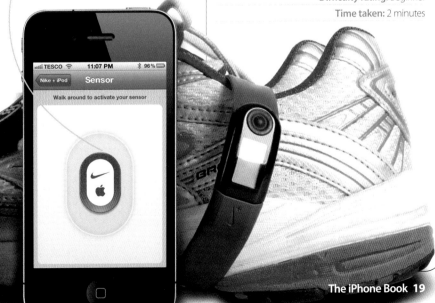

Top iPhone tips for…
Managing your media

The best ways to watch videos on the go

The iPhone isn't just a fantastic iPod, phone and web tool – it's also a brilliant way to watch TV and films on the move, or just to carry around your media in a tiny package. This is great if you have a bigger screen and an Apple TV, as it's now possible to use a Wi-Fi connection to view the movies you're carrying in your pocket on that larger display.

01 Using AirPlay
If you have an Apple TV, watch your favourite programmes and films wirelessly from your phone by connecting the two to the same Wi-Fi network. Navigate to the correct screen on the Apple TV, then start watching. A small icon should appear next to the video controls. Tap it and it will be sent to the screen to carry on watching.

Difficulty rating: Expert
Time taken: 10 minutes

02 AirPlay speakers
If you don't have an Apple TV, you don't have to miss out on the AirPlay action. All you need is an AirPlay-enabled speaker or two and you'll be able to pump the sound of your videos out of some powerful speakers, rather than simply out of your iPhone's tiny one or headphones. You can connect speakers through Wi-Fi or Bluetooth, if they have the functionality, and get some really powerful audio.

Difficulty rating: Beginner
Time taken: 5 minutes

"Watch TV and films on the move"

03 Home Sharing
If your iPhone's memory is full, you might not be able to add any videos to your device without deleting a lot of apps and music. However, this doesn't mean you can't watch content you've bought from iTunes. Enable Home Sharing on iTunes on your computer, as well as in the Videos section of the Settings app, and you can browse your iTunes library on your phone and watch films wirelessly.

Difficulty rating: Expert
Time taken: 10 minutes

04 Watch TV online
If you want to keep up with TV on the go, head to www.tvcatchup.com. You need to create an account to watch the channels, but it's completely free and very easy. Once you have an account you just have to tap the channel you want to watch to see what it's broadcasting live, and seeing as it works over 3G as well as Wi-Fi, you'll never need to worry about missing your top shows again.

Difficulty rating: Beginner
Time taken: 2 minutes

05 Filling the screen
Because of the way movies are made, they are often much wider than the screen of the iPhone, resulting in black bars at the top and bottom of the screen. If you would prefer to zoom in on the action and don't mind missing the edges, you can tap the arrow in the top-right of the screen or simply double-tap the picture to zoom in or out. Perfect for getting right into the heart of the action.

Difficulty rating: Beginner
Time taken: 1 minute

Top iPhone tips for...

Music

Our top tips for making the most of your tunes

O ne of the apps the iPhone has introduced since its launch is the Music app, which has provided all the functionality of Apple's bestselling music player in a device you can use to contact people online and via texts/phone calls. Here are a few tricks to make using your iPhone as an iPod far simpler and cooler than it was before.

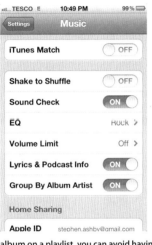

01 Sound check

Sometimes you may come across an album that you might have ripped from a CD, where the volume is much lower than your other tracks. If you use shuffle, or have a song from this album on a playlist, you can avoid having to turn the volume up and down constantly by heading into Settings>Music and turning on Sound Check. This will analyse the volume of each track you have and wll then set them all to the same level.

Difficulty rating: Beginner

Time taken: 2 minutes

03 Personalise your tabs

You can change the tabs along the bottom of the Music app window by selecting the More button and tapping Edit in the top-left. From here you can drag section headings from the grid at the top of the screen to the position you want along the bottom. This is great for speeding up your navigation around the Music app, as you can drag only the sections you use most into the bar.

Difficulty rating: Beginner

Time taken: 4 minutes

02 VoiceOver

When you're listening to a track you can find out what it is without ever needing to look at your phone using VoiceOver. Just hold down the Home button on your iPhone, or the Pause button on your headphones, and the phone will lower the music volume and speak to you with the track name and artist. If you have an iPhone 4S, you can do the same, but ask your device to fetch the same result.

Difficulty rating: Beginner

Time taken: 1 minute

05 Equalizer

Everyone has different music on their iPods, and depending on the headphones or speakers you're using, you might find that certain tracks have a little too much treble or bass. If this is the case, head into Settings, then choose the Music tab. Touch the EQ section and you can flick through different settings from Rock to Acoustic. Do this while a track is playing and you can compare modes to see which is best for you.

Difficulty rating: Beginner

Time taken: 5 minutes

04 Headphone genius

This tip isn't specifically something you can do, as it just happens automatically, but if you have more than one set of headphones or speakers, your iPhone will do something brilliant. Unplug one set of headphones and plug in another and your iPhone recognises which headphones you are using and changes the volume to the last level you set when you used those cans. Now that right there is what we call a smartphone.

Difficulty rating: Beginner

Time taken: 1 minute

"All the functionality of Apple's bestselling music player in a single device you can use to contact people online and via texts/ phone calls"

Getting started

The default applications explored

"Enjoy your magazine library all in one place"

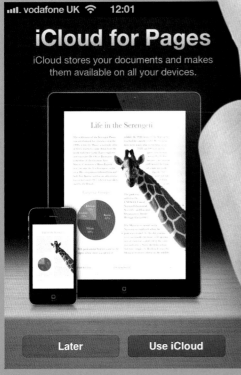

iCloud for Pages

iCloud stores your documents and makes them available on all your devices.

Later   Use iCloud

26 iCloud will change the way you use your iPhone forever

Understand the Settings

A guide to using the iPhone's Settings panel

The Settings app, as you'd expect, is where you can tweak and personalise the inner workings of your iPhone. Click on the cog icon, and you'll be transported to a control panel listing topics, from wallpapers to Wi-Fi, and everything else in between.

The 'General' tab houses the most commonly accessed and vital functions. Here, you can add and remove Wi-Fi networks, apply a password, amend the date and time, change the language and more.

Elsewhere, each header will directly relate to the app in its title, so selecting the Safari header, for example, will give you the chance to customise settings for web browsing, such as blocking pop-ups, clearing the history, and opting for your preferred internet search engine. Meanwhile, 'Music' offers you the chance to apply a volume limit or implement home sharing through your Apple ID.

If you want to change your email signature, your screen brightness or the iPhone's wallpaper, you can do it all in the Settings app.

> "Click on the cog icon and you will be transported to a control panel with topics from wallpapers to Wi-Fi"

● **Airplane Mode**
Switching this to 'On' disables the wireless features of your iPhone in order to comply with airline regulations

● **Wi-Fi**
Set up a Wi-Fi connection, delete one or remove it altogether for an offline iPhone experience

● **Notifications**
This is where your device alerts you to new messages, emails, etc. Customise your Notification Center here

● **Wallpaper**
Change the iPhone's appearance by using one of the default wallpaper images or one of your own photos

● **General**
Apply a password, set the date and time, activate Bluetooth or turn your sounds on or off here

---

Enable restrictions
Take control of your iPhone

If there's more than one person that will be using your iPhone – especially if it's a child or teenager who enjoys using apps at home – you might like to consider enabling restrictions to certain apps or functions.

If you would like to restrict certain privileges, selecting General>Restrictions in the Settings app will present a page of the most popular apps with settings to restrict. In the first

instance you will be asked to set a four-digit Passcode, and once that's done you'll be able to browse through the list of apps and select On/Off accordingly.

Possibly one of the most important areas for parents is the prevention of in-app purchases, and just a simple slide from On to Off in the Restrictions menu could prevent a hefty iTunes bill after a child's gaming session. Additionally, you can set

ratings that are relevant for the country that you're living in to prevent unsuitable apps, games, music, films or television shows being purchased by children or teenagers via the iTunes Store.

However, perhaps one of the best features of the Restrictions section is the ability to approve multiplayer games or adding friends – a vital feature for parents of children of all ages, we're sure you'll agree.

Key features
What you can do within this app

◀ Customise email settings
It's possible to have more than one email account accessible from your iPhone. To add or delete these, go to the 'Mail, Contacts and Calendar' section. While you're here, you can tweak how many recent messages you can view, whether you'd like to preview a line or two of these when they're displayed in a list, and also change the font size. For those who prefer to attach signatures, sync events or sort the order of your contacts, this can also be done in Mail.

◀ Customise appearance
You can customise the look of your device in Settings. Go to 'Brightness', and then either enable 'Auto Brightness' or move the slider to change the brightness of the screen (this can also help conserve battery power). You can also go to 'Wallpaper' and alter your Home or Lock screen appearance using stock images or your own photos from the Camera Roll or Photo Stream.

"Conserve your battery by lowering the brightness"

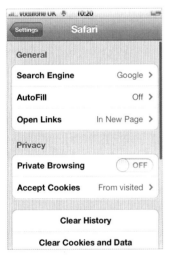

◀ Personalise browsing
To personalise your web-browsing options, go to the 'Safari' section in Settings. Here, choose from the most popular search engines to pick your preferred option, activate AutoFill to save typing time, and clear your History. You can also block pop-up adverts and receive warnings for if you stumble on a fraudulent site. These options give you full control over how you access the web.

▶ Your own personal iCloud
New to iOS 5 is the iCloud, your own personal cloud storage space. You are initially provided with 5GB of space for free, but you also have the option of purchasing more if you need it, as well as being able to sync all of your favourite apps to iCloud so that emails, contacts, calendars, bookmarks, notes and documents can be automatically saved to it. Furthermore, by using Photo Stream, iCloud will also push all of the photos taken on your iPhone to your other devices, such as your Mac.

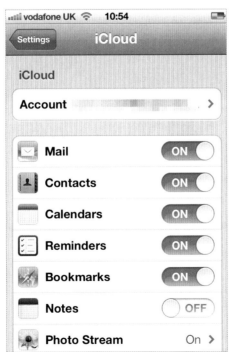

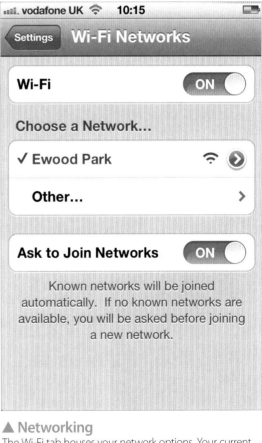

▲ Networking
The Wi-Fi tab houses your network options. Your current network – if you're hooked up to it – will be displayed in blue text. If you'd like to add another network, click on 'Other', and you can input new details and a password.

Back up and sync wirelessly with iCloud

Store your music, photos and files in your own virtual storage space

One of the best new additions to the iOS universe is, without question, iCloud. This service is free to all iOS 5 users, and is essentially 5GB of cloud storage space. There is no manual transferring of files or data to worry about, as your personal cloud simply hovers over you, soaking up and absorbing data, such as back-ups, photos, music files, documents, apps and so on, ensuring that everything you need is close at hand for times of need. By extension, there are many great services that become available thanks to this system, such as photos you take on your iPhone, or music files you download on your iPad being automatically pushed to all of your iOS devices so that everything is instantly accessible. You should definitely take time to learn about the merits of your iCloud and start using it straight away, as it will make your life easier, which is exactly what it was designed for.

"Your personal Cloud simply hovers over you, soaking up and absorbing data, such as back-ups, photos, music files, documents, apps and so on"

Your account
You have to enter your Apple ID and password to log in and start using your iCloud

App compatibility
You can determine which of your apps take advantage of iCloud

Find Device
Your iCloud can track your devices and pinpoint their locations on a map, so you'll never misplace your iPhone again

Storage
You get 5GB of iCloud storage space for free, and pay for additional space if you come to require it

Delete account
You can delete an iCloud account at any time, which is handy if you are passing your device on

Find your friends

Apple's new social networking app lets you stay connected to the people who matter

Working in the same way as the Find My iPhone app, Apple's new social networking app, Find My Friends, allows iOS users to meet up with their friends at outdoor concerts, keep track of their family on a day out and see when guests are close to arriving so that you can get the roast in the oven. With a classy interface, Find My Friends invites you to share your location with others across your iCloud, and vice versa, so that you can quickly see where they are and what they're up to on a map. You can choose to temporarily share your location with a group of people for a limited period of time, making it perfect for staying safe on a weekend rock climbing trip, go invisible with the flick of a switch and apply parental controls to ensure that your children never mistakenly divulge their location to any unsavoury types. The app is free to download and easy to set up, and as it compliments your Contacts and Maps apps, you can do some very cool things with it, like find the quickest route to a surprise party without bumping into the guest of honour. The possibilities, as they say, are endless.

Key features

What your iCloud can do for you

◀ Auto backup

Your personal iCloud backs up your device daily over Wi-Fi when it's connected to a power source. Once you plug it in, everything – including your music, photos, files and settings – is backed up quickly and efficiently. Not only does this provide sound peace of mind that your files will always be safe, but you can also restore an existing device or transfer all of your data to a new one by connecting the device to Wi-Fi and entering your Apple ID and password.

◀ Photo Stream

With Photo Stream, you can take a photo on one device and it will automatically appear on all of your other devices, including your Mac or PC. What's more, if you import pictures to your computer from a digital camera, iCloud will send copies of them to your iPhone or other device over Wi-Fi and you can also view your images on your TV via Apple TV without the need to sync or manually transfer the files.

"Take a photo and it will appear on your other devices"

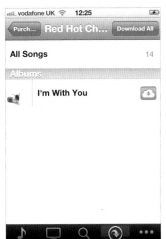

◀ iTunes in the Cloud

Long gone are the days when you had to drag all music and videos purchased from iTunes to your various devices in order to copy it across. With iCloud, you can have iTunes automatically download new music and purchases to all of your devices the moment you tap 'Buy'. With the iTunes app, you can also browse your purchase history, and choose songs, albums or shows to download again at no additional cost.

▶ Never lose your device again

If you download the free Find My iPhone app from Apple, you'll be able to track and locate your devices from any computer web browser in the event of your misplacing them. You will have the option to configure this feature when setting up iOS 5 on your device, but otherwise you can go to Settings, tap 'iCloud', and then enable the 'Find My iPhone' from there. Once set up, you can log into your iCloud from any computer and pinpoint the location of your device on a map.

▲ Documents in the Cloud

Thanks to the iCloud, you can keep your work up to date across all of your devices. Any changes you make will automatically appear on your other iOS devices, completely eradicating the need to transfer files.

Discover iTunes

Learning more about your very own music and media store

iTunes is an app that houses a whole range of music, films, television programmes, podcasts and audiobooks. If it's a particular artist, group, song or author you're looking for, you should be able to find them via the Search bar – type the name or keyword in and you're good to go. Additionally, the Featured and Top Charts tabs enable you to see the newly released singles, albums, films and TV shows.

The great thing about this app is that even if you're feeling a little uninspired musically or otherwise, you can activate the Genius function through your home Mac or PC and it'll offer a selection of recommendations based on your past purchases and download history.

Not only that, whether you're on a budget or have cash to splash, you're sure to find something here that'll suit your wallet. Podcasts are very often free and are searchable by category, 'new and noteworthy', or simply by you knowing what or who you're looking for.

"If you're feeling uninspired musically, you can activate the Genius function and it'll offer you recommendations based on your download history"

● **What's new?**
Newly released tracks, albums, films and more can be found by clicking here

● **Genres**
Narrow your search options with the Genre button in the top-left of the screen

● **Closer view**
Simply click on the view arrow to take a closer look at the product you have in mind – you can then buy from within this pop-up screen

● **Categories**
All of the content within iTunes is organised into categories, such as Music, Videos and More, which are viewable as icons along the bottom of the screen

● **Search**
The intelligent search feature ensures you're able to look for what you want when you need it

---

Learn with iTunes U

A fantastic education resource at your fingertips

A rather excellent addition to this app is iTunes U for learning resources that are searchable by subject or educational institution. This collection – or, rather, library – of discussions and more enables individuals to start or continue their education via their iPhone. Many of them are free and could be of use whether you're studying or just eager to expand your knowledge on a new topic.

The Featured tab offers a hot pick of the latest resources uploaded; meanwhile the Top Charts provide a snapshot of the most popular files. With highly regarded institutions such as Oxford University, Stanford and more providing content, it's an excellent opportunity to indulge in some higher education.

Learn how to build a business, tackle iPhone Application Development, or Astronomy.

If that doesn't take your fancy search for a topic that does. The choice is yours. Meanwhile, clicking on Beyond Campus will take you to a drop-down list of institutions such as museums, theatres and organisations like the British Council offering advice and expertise on a range of topics. And the best thing about it? You don't have to be a student to partake in it. What are you waiting for?

Key features

Heading beyond the interface

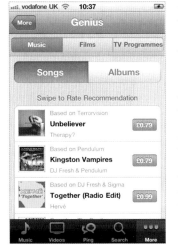

◀ Recommendations

The iTunes' Genius function recommends new music, film, television shows and more media entertainment based on your own existing and previous purchases and downloads. While it requires activation via your home Mac or PC, once you've done this, there will be a whole range of new media available for you to choose from. It's ideal if you're looking to expand your tastes in the areas you enjoy and explore new avenues of entertainment.

◀ Discover new music

The Ping function is another great way to find out about new music and network with friends and other fellow iTunes Store users. Ping enables you to follow your favourite artists or friends to find out what they're listening to, raving about or downloading. While you'll need to activate it within iTunes 10 on your Mac or PC, once that's done the button on your iPhone will ensure its functionality is, quite literally, at your fingertips.

"Ping enables you to follow your favourite artists or friends"

◀ View Downloads

Pressing the More tab at the bottom of the iTunes window and choosing Downloads will take you to the track, album, movie or more that you're currently downloading or content that's queued for download. The latest version of the iTunes Store's Terms and Conditions is also viewable here – click on it to view a page full of each country's relevant Ts and Cs in case you need to refer to them.

▶ Get the best bits

Podcasts are essentially audible programmes featuring some of your favourite comedians, radio presenters and more. Some are condensed versions of radio shows – others have been specially recorded for the iTunes Store. The majority of them are free, which means you can stock up on listening content without having to worry about your bank account. If there's something you've particularly enjoyed you can also subscribe to this podcast so that future recordings will automatically be lined up for you to listen to.

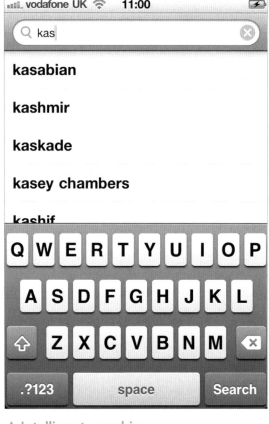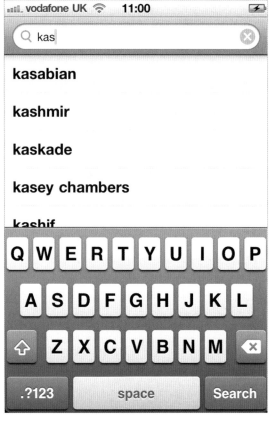

▲ Intelligent searching

Your iTunes app includes a comprehensive search engine. By simply typing the first letter or two of a name, a list of possibilities are presented with the most popular choices at the top. Scroll through to find the one you're looking for.

Get to know the App Store

We take a closer look at this interactive storefront

The App Store effectively acts as a separate storefront in which you can stock up on fun, informative or entertaining applications for your iPhone. Much like the iTunes Store, you can search by newly released apps or popular recommendations from other users. Additionally, by setting up the Genius function with the app, you'll be presented choices that are tailored to your previous downloads or purchases.

These apps can range in quality and type from the bizarre to the downright useful, but the price varies on each. While there are a large number of free apps, other paid-for programmes can offer free trials or 'lite' versions for you to enjoy. The rating system also provides another way for you to research just how good a product is before you potentially waste your hard drive space, or worse, hard-earned cash on a sub-standard app. You can also view any updates that are relevant to apps that you've purchased in the past right here, too.

> "The apps on sale in the App Store can range in quality and type from the bizarre to the downright useful"

New
Browse through the apps by release date, 'what's hot', or the new ones on offer

Genius
The Genius button introduces you to new apps that you'll love, judging by past downloads

Updates
Click on the Updates icon to see if any of your apps have now been improved

Search tab
Know what you're looking for? Type the name in the Search bar to access it quickly

---

Contact customer services
Get a little extra help when you need it

Most of the time, we have no doubt that your experiences shopping with and browsing the App Store will be enjoyable and problem-free; however, it's always best to be prepared in case something unforeseen crops up.

Luckily for us Apple customers, its support centre is packed full of helpful information, including a wide selection of discussion forums, video tutorials and lists of popular topics that you can easily access simply by clicking on the Support button, which is located at the bottom of the main screen.

So, for example, if you have tried to redeem an iTunes voucher code that's turned out to be invalid, need to find your lost tracks or downloaded shows, or you just have a couple of questions about your iTunes bill, then have a look through this large selection of troubleshooting tips, where there's a good chance that your query will be satisfactorily covered in a good amount of detail.

Alternatively, if you still can't find the answer that you're looking for, simply send an email to Apple, and you should receive a response to your question within 24 hours. It's really quite straightforward.

Key features
The App Store highlights

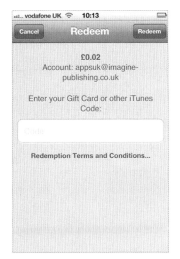

◀ Redeem your voucher
If you've purchased or have been given an iTunes voucher as a gift, then you will be able to redeem it through the App Store interface. Don't worry if you'd like to spread it across music and app purchases, as the money will be credited to your iTunes account so that you can spend the cash as you see fit. Simply click on 'Redeem' (at the bottom of the 'Featured' page) and enter the code.

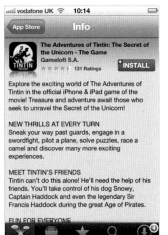

◀ Purchase apps
As you would expect, the App Store enables you to purchase and download products that you like the look of. You can search by the name – if you know it – with the 'Search' tab at the bottom of the screen, or browse through the 'Top 25' categories or 'Featured' selections – there's a whole wealth of content out there just waiting to be downloaded and used.

"Purchase and download products you like the look of"

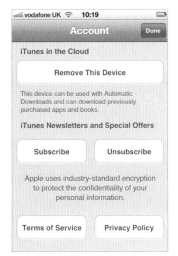

◀ Access your iTunes account
You can look at and amend your account details as you see fit by tapping on your account at the bottom of the 'Featured' page. If you need to change your debit card details or email address, it can all be done here. Additionally, if you want to log out of your account – which is a good idea if you're using your device to keep the kids entertained – you can also do it right here.

▶ Purchase history
A new tab at the top of the Updates window allows you to view your entire purchase history for the account that you are logged in on, meaning that you can re-download apps that may not be available to purchase as new in the App Store any more, as well as having the option to tap on the iCloud icon in order to push them to your other devices. It's a handy and useful new feature that ensures that you'll always have a record of what you've bought, which could be handy in a variety of circumstances.

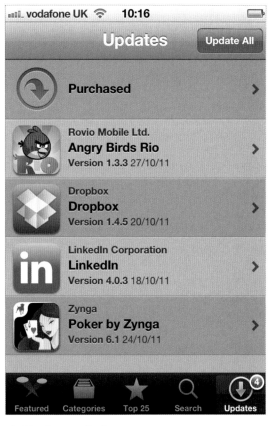

▲ Update existing apps
From time to time, the apps you've downloaded will be updated. You'll be alerted to updates by a number in a red circle on the Updates icon. You can scroll through the list, read the amendments, then update as you wish.

Explore Safari

Your essential guide to web browsing on the iPhone

Safari is your window to the worldwide web on your iPhone. Here, you've got the internet at your fingertips and you can scroll through webpages using your digits, or zoom by pinching and expanding your fingers – it's an intuitive system that works brilliantly.

Another great thing is you can have multiple windows open at the same time and toggle through them all with the tap of a button, which is great for switching to chosen sites whenever you need to, eradicating the need to rely on the forward or back buttons that you will find in your desktop version of Safari. If you click on a site's image with a zoom function, it will more often than not open into a new window by default, so as not to overcomplicate or clutter your iPhone's browsing abilities.

In the same way that you'd bookmark your favourite sites or pages of note, you can also save them to your Home screen, whereby they become like app icons and you can tap on them to launch the Safari app and jump straight to your favourite page in seconds. Thanks to the iOS 5 update, which you can install for free by connecting your device up to iTunes, there are also loads of great extra features to enjoy, such as Reading List and Reader, two neat additions that let you save your favourite articles to read later and read articles free from unnecessary clutter and pop-up ads.

> "Safari is your window to the worldwide web. You have the internet at your fingertips"

Web URL
If you know which website you're looking for, simply type the URL/ web address into the middle bar, and click Go

Search
Use the Search bar, top-right of the page, to look for the website or topic you have in mind

Open pages
All your open pages will show as separate windows that you can scroll through and select by tapping this icon

Tabs
Favourite websites, or ones which you view regularly, can be stored on your Home screen to make it quicker and easier to access. Tap the arrow icon to set these

Bookmarks
Access or edit bookmarks by pressing the button at the bottom of the screen

---

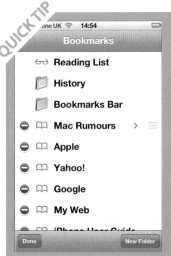

Use the bookmarks
Organise your favourite sites

The internet has a whole variety of uses for us in our day-to-day and working lives, so it's understandable that bookmarking a few of those is a great way to save time in the future. However, having a whole load of bookmarked sites can eventually get out of hand.

To prevent this situation, it's wise to implement a systematic approach to bookmarking in the first instance. By creating folders

with recognisable names, you can access those handy pages when you really need them, rather than trawling through a long list of confusing URLs that you've long-since forgotten.

If you click on the open book icon along the bottom of the Safari browser window, you'll be presented with a Bookmarks bar, which you can either use to select Bookmarks, or Edit. By clicking on Edit, you can create lots of

different folders with helpful names, such as News, Gift Ideas, Cool Exhibitions and so on. Then when you come to bookmark your sites (press the arrow icon and select from the drop-down list when you're on your site of choice), you can select the destination folder that it should sit in. Taking a few minutes to organise your bookmarks will save you a lot of time in the long run and is well worth the effort.

Key features

The functions of this browsing app

◀ Visit websites

As you'd expect, this internet-browsing app enables you to check out webpages at your leisure. While sites with Flash functionality won't work on your device – iPhones don't support Flash, unfortunately – overall, it shouldn't affect your browsing experience too much. Surprisingly, the size of the screen is in no way an obstacle when browsing webpages, you simply pinch and expand your fingers on the screen to zoom in and make them easier to read.

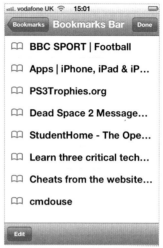

◀ Bookmarks

In the same way that your favourite sites can be bookmarked for future use, the Safari app lets you do this too. If you click on the open book symbol along the bottom bar of the screen, you'll be presented with a list. Within that list you can edit and organise your bookmarked pages, or add new ones to it. See the Quick Tip boxout to find out more.

"You can edit and organise your book-marked pages or add new ones to your list"

◀ Search and go

The bar on the top-right of the screen enables you to search for a topic or website by typing it in. You can use one of three search engine providers – this can be changed within the Safari tab when you click on Settings – but it's set to Google by default. It'll make suggestions as soon as you type the first letter; it will also list more recent searches in case they're relevant too.

▶ Reader

There are some great new Safari enhancements that have become available with the iOS 5 update, such as Reader, a handy feature that allows you to read articles that have had all of the unnecessary ads and page furniture stripped out. Whenever you open a webpage that is compatible with Reader, a distinctive 'Reader' logo will appear in the address bar. Tap this and the article will be stripped back to its purest form, making it easier for you to read without having distractions peppered all over the page. A simple idea, but a very good one.

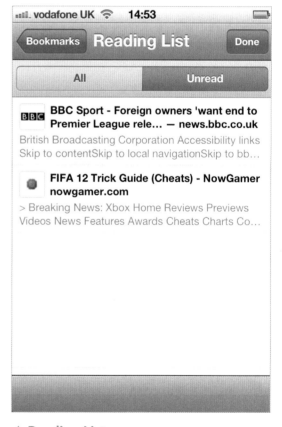

▲ Reading List

This Reading List allows you to save articles to our own personal list to continue reading later, even offline, and you can also start reading an online article on one device and, using iCloud, finish it on another later on.

Use Mail on the iPhone

All your emails on one handy app

Mail on the iPhone is a simple way to access your emails without having to always face a login screen and enter a password. Once it's set up you can view all your mailboxes in one place at just a press of a button from the home screen. So if you have lots of email accounts on the go, such as personal and work accounts, then by entering all of the account details you'll get messages from all of your accounts streamed into one inbox.

Your inbox is displayed in one long easy-to-read column and when you tap on a message it'll appear full-screen so that you can read it clearly. Managing your emails is simple too – just select the Edit button and you can tick off which messages to delete, archive or move into other folders. One of the other great things about Mail is that your number of new messages is viewable from the number in the red circle on the Home screen icon, thus instantly alerting you to the arrival of any new messages. So rather than launch the app and continuously tap the refresh button, you can just relax and wait for a visual cue before launching the app.

"Your inbox is displayed in one long, easy-to-read column and when you tap on a message it'll appear in full screen"

Mailboxes
This displays everything, from your inbox to the trash, spam and your named folders

Edit
Click on Edit and you'll be able to archive or move your emails to your dedicated folders

Flag messages
Add a 'flag' to highlight messages that are important or for you to read fully at a later date

Refresh
To refresh the contents of you inbox and download all new messages, tap the arrow button

Compose
Tap on the pen and paper icon to call up a fresh email window into which you can compose a new message

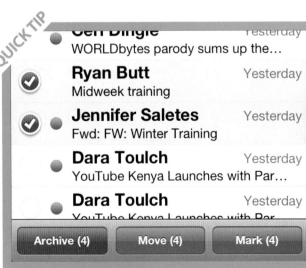

Clear out your inbox

Take charge of all those emails with the Edit function

An unruly inbox is common, but it does make it extremely difficult to spot the important messages from the spam and nonsense. Don't worry, though, there are ways to cut it down to size. One way is to select the Edit function within the mailbox you want to organise – we decided to tackle the inbox. Once you've done that you'll have a circle appear down the left-hand side of your message column – ditching some of the spam in bulk will clear the space a lot quicker.

As soon as you select the message it'll have a red tick by the side of it and they'll start forming a little pile in the right-hand panel. Keep going as many times as necessary and then press the blue 'Move' button. Select Trash and away they go. In order to keep the messages down in the future, you could also file some in the Spam folder.

Key features
Five things the Mail app does

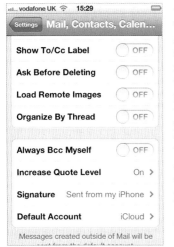

◀ Receive mail

You can link up any of your existing email addresses to the Mail app via the iPhone's Settings app. You'll need all the relevant details, including passwords and so on to do this, but once it's all set up you'll be able to view it from the icon on the Home screen. There are other things to change in the Mail, Contacts, Calendars section, including your email signature (set to 'Sent from my iPhone' by default) and the number of messages shown.

◀ Edit mailbox

Just like the online mailbox functions you use through your chosen internet browser, you can edit your various mailboxes – inbox, junk, sent and so on – as you wish. Whether you use these mailboxes for deleting your unwanted messages or archiving them for future use, it can all be done here. It's something to consider if you want to keep your inboxes organised and under control.

"You can link up any of your existing email addresses"

◀ Set up an account

Click on the Settings icon from the Home screen, select 'Mail, Contacts, Calendars', to see the header 'Accounts' at the top of the screen. Select 'Add Account', select the email account – Gmail, Yahoo!, AOL and so on – and input the details. If you have more than one account, you can view them all within this app – perfect to channel all emails into one handy inbox.

▶ Enter contacts

There are a couple of ways that you can input your recipient's details into an email – the first way is to just type it, but if you simply type the first letter you'll be presented with a drop-down list of contacts that could match who you're after. It's one of the many time-saving features included in Mail. Alternatively, you can press on the '+' symbol in the top-right corner and then choose from your saved contacts. So it also pays to organise your contacts into easy-to-find categories to speed up the process further.

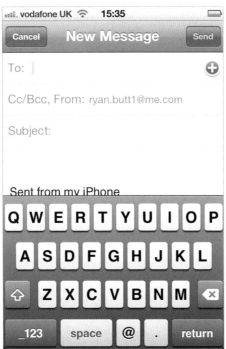

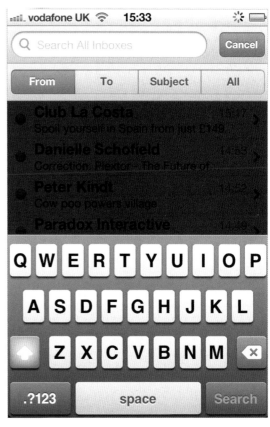

▲ Search mail

If you haven't yet got round to filing your emails into their respective folders the Search function is helpful. Type in a keyword and the app will do the rest for you. You also have the option of checking on the mail server too.

Understand the Calendar

Your all-in-one organisational tool

Tuesday 9 Calendar is one of those apps that if you put a bit of time into mastering and understanding it, you will find it completely invaluable. This is because it acts as a planner, scheduler, reminder and diary all in one. Its features enable you to view it in a variety of formats, each allowing for more and more detail to be added. So if you like to have your days planned to perfection, hour by hour, then this is definitely for you. On the flip-side, for those with a bad memory for dates, pop in all your anniversaries and birthdays (which are picked up from Contacts anyway), and set them to repeat and alert annually, meaning you have no excuses. The Calendar can be synced with all your portable devices and with other non-Apple organisers too, so you only need to keep one up to date, and the rest will have the information at the next sync. If you are using iOS 5 then your personal iCloud allows information on your iPhone calendar to be synced to your cloud and then updated on your iPad or Mac calendar within seconds of adding them – you don't even have to save anything. It's the ultimate planning tool.

"For those of you with a bad memory for dates, pop in all anniversaries and birthdays and set to repeat annually"

● **Calendars**
Tap this button to view all of the calendars that are currently active and synced to your device

● **Add Event**
Click the '+' button to add a new event to the Calendar

● **Today**
The Today tab lets you switch back to the current day in an instant

● **View**
Hit these tabs along the bottom of the window to choose your Calendar view

---

Explore the in-depth views
See your Calendar three different ways

There are three view options on the iPhone's Calendar selected from the menu across the bottom of the screen. The Month view provides an at-a-glance perspective of any calendar month and by tapping on a specific day you are presented with the list of events, if any, that correspond with that date at the bottom of the window. The Day view is the most like your standard diary, so

you can write in personal notes and thoughts for each day as required by tapping the '+' icon in the top-right corner of the screen. The final view is List, which gives you a full list of upcoming events to scroll through. This works best in landscape orientation, as you can view up to three days at a time, making it easy to see what you have lined up for the current day and those that follow immediately after. Using Calendar

is most productive when using all of these views, as you can ditch the paper diary completely, plus it syncs with all the other system apps in a way that's ultra-intuitive. If you have more than one Apple device on the go, such as an iPhone and iPad, then you can set your personal iCloud to sync your calenders, so that when something is added to one, it is added to all of them within seconds. Now that's clever.

Key features

How to use to the app to its best ability to organise your life

◀ Add Calendars

In Month view, your Calendar serves as the essential monthly planner, with all of your plans shown by day. You can add different calendars for keeping your personal and work engagements separate, and any birthday dates that you have stored in your Contacts listings have their own Calendar, so you don't need to input these again. Click on any event in order to see more information you've input about it, such as start and end times and locations.

◀ Add new event

It's easy to add a new event to your Calendar. First, hit the '+' button to bring up the New Event dialogue. Here, you can add the start and end times of the meeting, the location, whether it repeats or not (say for anniversaries and the like), meaning that you only have to input it once. There is also a Notes section that enables you to add further information about an event.

"Add different calendars to keep work separate"

◀ Search for events

As with all the built-in System apps, there is a Search field (available in the 'List' tab). By typing in here, you will be presented with a list of all the events that match your search. These are presented in chronological order, and you can tap an event to go to that day and see more information. If you have a lot of dates, using the Notes field will help to narrow things down.

▶ Set Alerts

When there are a lot of events it can get be difficult to remember to check in with your Calendar to see what's coming up in the next week or so. Luckily, you can set an Alert either when you create the event or by editing it afterwards, which will remind you any time from five minutes before up to two days before, so you know what's happening and when with plenty of warning. This will work in conjunction with your Notification Center so that you will never be out of the loop as to what's going on in your life.

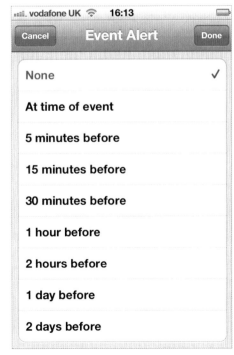

▲ Schedule birthdays

Birthdays have their own calendar in the app, and this is synced from your Contacts database. That will automatically now show up in Calendar to save you having to retype all those details again.

Keep in touch with Contacts

Have all your essential contact details at a tap

Contacts is your on-the-go address book that helps you to stay up to date and in touch with your friends and family wherever you are. It looks like a standard print address book, with lettered tabs down the right-hand side and a full list of all your contacts. When you select a contact, you see all of that person's details in full on the right. As well as storing the usual phone numbers and addresses, Contacts enables you to add photos, notes, multiple addresses, websites, email addresses and more. All your contacts can be grouped, so that your personal and work contacts, for example, can be kept separately. There's plenty of additional fields that you can add too, such as birthdays, job titles, IM addresses, middle names and so on, so it is perfect to use as a networking tool. Like so many other apps on your device, information from Contacts is also used in other apps, such as Calendar, so it definitely pays to input as much information as possible because you'll never know when it may come in handy elsewhere on your device.

"All your contacts can be grouped, so that work and personal contacts can be kept separate, for example"

Edit
Hit the 'Edit' icon on the right of the screen to make changes to an existing contact

Map
Tap on an address in your contacts book to get directions in Maps instantly

Share
You can share a contact with other people easily by tapping the 'Share Contact' button

---

Customise your contacts

It's not just an address book

As well as storing people's **phone numbers, you can add supplementary detail about a person to Contacts, making it a complete organiser.** We've already mentioned that you can add photos to a person's profile, but you can also list a person's iPhone number so that you can make the most of the FaceTime feature. There are fields for all the usual essential details, like address and email, but to really make the most of this app, make sure that you use the additional fields too. This lets you put in a birthday for your contact, which you can be reminded of via the Calendar. You can also add things like Nicknames or Job Titles, which help you remember more about the people on your phone. When you have a detailed contact, you can also choose to share it with others by hitting the Share button underneath any contact. This will attach a VCF file to an email so that it can be sent to anyone who might need it. Like pretty much every standard app on your device, Calendar stores and shares information with other apps to ensure that every rough edge of your busy life is smoothed away making even the most mundane of tasks simple. So it pays to keep your contacts updated with every ounce of info.

Key features

It's more than just an address book

◀ Add a contact

Adding new contacts to your ever-expanding database is easy. Open your Contacts book in the Phone app and then tap the '+' icon in the top-right corner. You will then be presented with a comprehensive page of fields you can apply data to, including the obvious names and phones numbers through to company info, postal and email addresses. Tap on a field and you will be able to enter whatever information you know.

◀ Put a face to a name

You can easily add a photo to a person's contact details using the Add photo command when you open a contact for editing. This will default to the photo albums stored on your iPhone. Open a contact and then choose the 'Edit' option, then tap on 'Add Photo' and choose a picture from your device. Then move the image around the screen and pinch or expand to scale it, then tap 'Choose' to add it to the contact.

"You can easily add a photo to a person's contact details"

▶ Search contacts

There is a dedicated Search engine at the top of your contacts list, which you can use to find people without having to manually flick through – essential if your number of contacts is getting unwieldy. Start typing any part of the contact's name and a list of potential matches will pop up for you to select from. If you see the one you want, simply scroll down to highlight the contact and then select it. It's a very intuitive, handy system that saves a lot of time, especially if you're popular.

◀ Get directions

With so many addresses in one place it can be easy to get lost. With Contacts, you can tap an address to be taken to the Maps application, from which you can see the address, get directions and figure out how long it will take you to get there. It works in both directions too; if you find a service, for example, in Maps, you can add it directly to your Contacts.

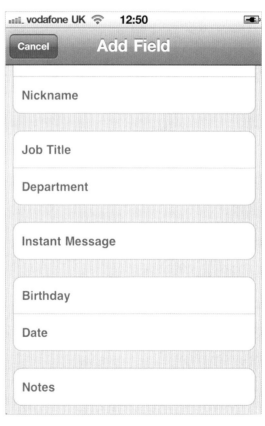

▲ Add extra fields

The Add Fields option brings up a long list of additional items that can be added to a contact. This includes their company and job title details, IM address, their birthday and much more.

Make calls on your iPhone

Everything you need to know to keep in touch using your device

Above all of the other fantastic functions and features that your iPhone provides, it is, first and foremost, just that – a phone. It also happens to be a very good phone, with a host of great intuitive features to make the act of making phone calls as simple and as painless as possible.

To make calls you simply tap the 'Keypad' option and enter all numbers manually, or you can store numbers that you use regularly in your Contacts so that they are all stored alphabetically for easy access – you simply tap on a contact to open their info page and then tap on a number to call it. If someone is calling you on your iPhone then there is no danger of you picking it up by mistake or cancelling the call as you fumble around for your phone in your pocket. When a call is incoming a slider will appear on your screen that you must physically move to take the call. Also, any calls that you happen to miss will be impossible to ignore because a message will appear on your screen informing you of a missed call and alerts appear next to your Phone app icon. Here we highlight some of the key functions of your Phone app and get you used to the art of managing your calls.

> "Any calls that you miss will be impossible to ignore, as a message will appear on screen"

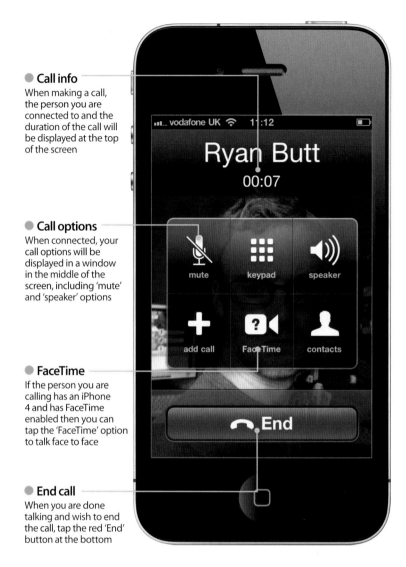

Call info
When making a call, the person you are connected to and the duration of the call will be displayed at the top of the screen

Call options
When connected, your call options will be displayed in a window in the middle of the screen, including 'mute' and 'speaker' options

FaceTime
If the person you are calling has an iPhone 4 and has FaceTime enabled then you can tap the 'FaceTime' option to talk face to face

End call
When you are done talking and wish to end the call, tap the red 'End' button at the bottom

---

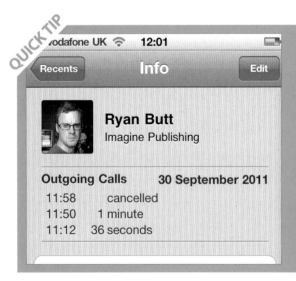

Monitor your call activity
Get to grips with your log to keep track of calls

To monitor your call activity, and to help prepare you for the event of a hefty bill, simply open your Phone app and then tap the 'Recents' option at the bottom of the screen. All incoming and outgoing calls will be listed – as well as any calls you happened to miss (tap the 'Missed' tab at the top of the screen to get the full rundown). Simply browse the list to get the numbers and the day or date they were called and tap the blue arrow to the right of individual entries to get more specific details. On this screen you will get a history of all calls made to that particular number as well as the duration of the calls. If the calls took place with someone in your Contacts then all of that particular person's contact details will also be displayed on the screen. If the number is unknown then you can create a new contact for that person on the same screen too, saving you vital time as you switch between options within your Phone app.

Key features

Explore the various options for managing calls

◀ Make a call

Making simple calls from your iPhone is easy. If you are dialling an original number (that isn't yet stored in your Contacts) then tap the 'Keypad' option at the bottom of the screen and a full telephone keypad will be displayed on your screen. Simply enter the number you wish to call, complete with area code, and then press the 'Call' button. To end a call, just press the red 'End' button and your phone will automatically return to your Home screen.

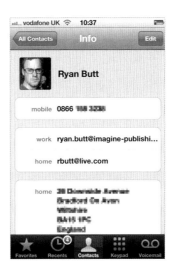

◀ Call someone from your Contacts

If you have a number stored in your Contacts that you would like to call then tap the 'Contacts' option at the bottom of the screen and then scroll through your alphabetical list until you find the person in question. Once the contact is opened, tap on the number you have entered for that person and your iPhone will automatically start calling them. Again, tap the red 'End' button to cancel the call.

"Tap a number on a website to call it"

◀ Call from a website

If you are looking up a phone number from a website you don't have to write down the number or even copy and paste it. Any numbers on websites should be highlighted as a link, so tap on them and the option to call the number should then be displayed. Choose 'Call' and your phone will automatically dial the number. Press the red 'End' button to cancel the call as normal.

▶ Make conference calls

If you need to make a conference call – making a call to someone that other people in the room can hear and are privy to – then you can activate your phone's loudspeaker at any time during a phone call by tapping the 'Speaker' button that is displayed among your call options when your current call is in progress. You may need to adjust the volume on the side of your device so that everyone can hear the call well enough. All you need to do is tap the same option again to deactivate the loudspeaker.

▲ Mute a call

There may be times that you need to mute a call, just tap the 'Mute' button that is displayed among your call options when your current call is in progress. Tap it again to return to normal.

Get to know Messages

Everything you need to know to get started with Apple's chat service

Apple's Message app has always been the most efficient texting service around due to its functionality and ease of use. You can send media files like pictures using this app and the good news is that Apple has improved the service further with iMessage. This allows you to send text messages to fellow iMessage users absolutely free over Wi-Fi or 3G networks.

Boasting an intuitive interface, you access the recipient from your Contacts or type in their phone number or email address (whatever is registered to their iMessage account), and then exchange texts via colour-coded speech bubbles in the main window. You can invite others to participate in group conversations and send photographs or videos from your device as attachments, which will also be displayed in the main window for others to view and comment on.

The app also works in conjunction with your personal iCloud, so if you start an iMessage conversation on one particular device, you can continue it on another later, picking up exactly where you left off.

"You can send text messages between devices absolutely free over Wi-Fi or 3G"

● Edit
You can delete messages by tapping the Edit button at the top of the window, and then individually select messages to erase

● Add media
Images and videos can be added and attached to messages. Just type your message, then tap the camera icon to select and send media

● Instant messaging
Sending messages is easy; just tap on the text field, type what you want, then hit the 'Send' button

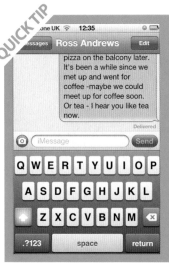

Understand delivery notifications

How to ensure that your messages get delivered… and read

One of the more subtle, but nevertheless useful benefits of using iMessage is that there is no way you can miss a message. Likewise, there is no excuse for others not to reply claiming that they didn't receive the message, because the app uses delivery receipts to provide confirmation that (a) your messages have actually been delivered to the intended recipient, and (b) that the person

who received the message actually read it. Confirmation of delivery is supplied automatically via a simple message that says 'Delivered' under your sent messages. To get confirmation that the people on the devices you're sending your messages to have read the messages, go to Settings from your Home screen, and then move the slider next to the text that reads 'Send Read Receipts' to 'On'. In Settings, you

also have the option to add email addresses to which incoming messages that will be delivered, as well as activate the option to have subject fields included with each message. Aside from that, the settings are as basic as the app itself, leaving you with nothing else to worry about except for texting until your thumbs go numb with fellow iOS 5 users. Talk has never been so cheap.

Key features

Communicating has never been so easy

◀ Group chat

Conversations in iMessage can take place between two people or groups of people; simply choose a recipient, type some text, and hit 'Send'. Each message will appear in speech bubbles in the main window, and are colour coded (each person has their own colour), so you can instantly see who said what. After sending a message, you can see if a response is incoming thanks to an ellipses icon at the bottom of the screen.

◀ Share media files

Communicating through Messages is a great way to share your photos and videos. When typing a message, hit the camera icon to the side of the text field, and then browse through your Camera Roll and choose pictures and video files to embed and share with the people you are conversing with. Images will be displayed within the message window, so other people don't have to open them up in a separate app to view attachments.

"Messages is great for sharing photos"

▶ Manage your messages

If you have Message conversations with certain people that you wish to keep secret from prying eyes – like if you're in the process of organising a surprise party, for instance – then you can manually manage, delete or forward certain messages from your list to other people. All you have to do is tap 'Edit' button on the top bar, and then review your message list and highlight specific messages in order to delete or forward messages by placing a tick in the circle.

◀ Easy typing and autocorrect

The iPhone features one of the most effective keypads around, which makes texting quick and easy. Responsive to the touch, you tap out what you want to write, and you don't even have to bother with punctuation, as your device will correct mistakes and insert apostrophes if you miss them out. Just keep an eye on those auto-corrections if you happen to mispell a word.

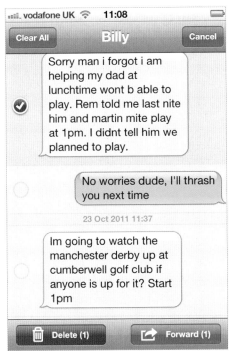

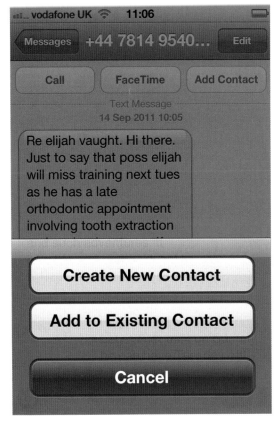

▲ App integration

The default apps on your iPhone work together and share information. To add and update contacts through Messages, tap 'Add Contact', and you will bring up a Contact sheet for the person you are communicating with.

Stay informed with Notification Center

Thanks to the new alerts system in iOS 5, you'll never miss a thing

As you will have already discovered through countless hours of using your device, you get notified of all kinds of different things through your iPhone, such as emails, app updates, friend requests and game announcements. Some are non-intrusive and take the form of little red numbers that sit on the app icons themselves, others are prominent messages that flash up in the middle of the screen, disrupting whatever it is you are currently doing. However, with Notification Center, it is possible to set your alerts to be small, non-intrusive banners that flash up at the top of the screen without interrupting what you are doing and, better still, you can swipe down from the top of the screen to see all of your alerts grouped together in one place, making it impossible to miss a thing. If you also decide that one of you alerts takes precedent over whatever it is you are currently doing (such as the movements on the Stock Market), you can take action by tapping on the actual alert and going straight to the app for more information.

> "With Notification Center it is possible to set your alerts to be non-intrusive banners that flash up at the top of the screen"

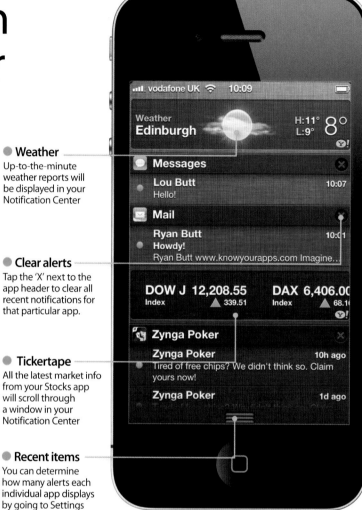

Weather
Up-to-the-minute weather reports will be displayed in your Notification Center

Clear alerts
Tap the 'X' next to the app header to clear all recent notifications for that particular app.

Tickertape
All the latest market info from your Stocks app will scroll through a window in your Notification Center

Recent items
You can determine how many alerts each individual app displays by going to Settings

Choose your alerts

Tailoring the settings to suit your individual needs

By exploring the Notifications options in Settings, you can modify the behaviour and contents of Notification Center. You have full freedom to dictate how you want an app to notify you by determining if it plays a sound, displays an app icon badge or whether it notifies you at all, as there will undoubtedly be a stack of apps – probably the kids' – on your device that you need never receive

notifications from. Essentially you can go through all of the apps on your device that send push notifications and then change their individual options – such as the number of recent items displayed for that app in your Notification Center, the style of alert it sends out (a non-intrusive banner at the top of the screen, an old-style alert or none at all), whether it displays badges or plays sounds and whether it will

appear on your Lock Screen. As you go through your apps, keep a close eye on the options available, because apps such as Messages feature additional options, such as 'Repeat Alert', which determines the number of times the app notifies you – just in case you miss the initial banner alert. By spending a little time going through the options you can tailor them to suit your own specific needs and lifestyle.

Key features

Taking push notifications to a whole new level of convenience

◀ Get a notification rundown

The main aspect of Notification Center is the way in which you can swipe down from the top of the screen, regardless of which app you are using, and get a complete rundown of all your recent notifications. This is very useful for seeing if you have missed or need to respond to any important emails or texts and for getting a bite-sized rundown of any pressing matters. Swipe up again to close the Notification Center.

◀ Jump straight to your apps

When using Notification Center, the alerts that you receive serve as launch pads, as well as visual indications that actions are required. Simply tap your finger on the alert and you will be instantly taken into the app in question so that you can conduct your actions. It saves the time and hassle of closing the alert, finding the app on your various Home screens and launching it, as was the case in previous operating systems.

"Simply tap your finger on the alert to go to the app"

◀ Clear alerts

You can edit the alerts in your Notification Center. If you get a list of alerts for a particular app that aren't too pressing, tap on the 'X' icon in the app header and then opt to 'Clear' the list of alerts for that app, paving the way for a fresh new batch that may need acting upon more urgently. It's an intuitive system that enables you to constantly stay in the loop of your life.

▶ Prioritise your alerts

You can tailor your own personal Notification Center by going to the Settings menu and changing the default. Here you can select the style in which your alerts are presented, whether they are likely to be urgent enough to be displayed on your Lock Screen and, best of all, the number of recent items that are displayed for each app in your Notification Center. So if you use the email function often in your line of work, it is possible for you to select to have up to 20 of the most recent ones displayed in your on-screen Notification Center.

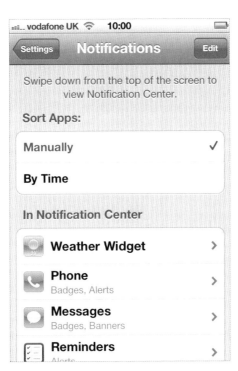

▲ Lock screen alerts

When your device is not in use, tap on a notification and then swipe your finger to the right to unlock your device and be taken straight to the app. This saves you a lot of time unlocking your device and finding the app.

Never forget with Reminders

The app that remembers everything, so you don't have to

Reminders lets you organise your life into 'To Do' lists, complete with due dates, notes and regular reminders from your device to ensure that you never get a bad dose of the scatter-brains when something important is pressing. With this app you simply jot down tasks, get your device to remind you when you need to do them by and then you simply tick each one off as you complete it. What's more, you can sync tasks between devices with iCloud – so when you add a new task on your iPhone, it will already be added to your list in the Reminders app on your iPad or iPod touch. With this simple and intuitive app it is impossible to miss a deadline, forget an important date or neglect to pick up some groceries again because whatever tasks you log into the app, it will remind you and alert you to the fact that you need to get them done. It's just another cool way in which your iOS device can make your life easier.

"You can sync tasks between devices using iCloud so that any new tasks will show on all of your iOS devices…"

Overview
By tapping the calendar icon you can get a complete overview of any calendar month and search for tasks

Change view
You can view your tasks as a simple list or broken down into days, making it easier to track what you have to do on a day-to-day basis

Tick list
When you successfully complete a task then you can tick it off. This makes it easy to keep track of your current goals

Your lists
All of your tasks are arranged as a straightforward list that you can refer to and tick off tasks as you complete them

Sync it to your cloud
Transfer tasks between devices

We have already mentioned how tasks in your Reminders app are automatically added to your Calendars app, but the magic doesn't stop there because you can also backup your tasks to your iCloud and get them synced across devices.

What this means is that if you have iOS 5 installed on both your iPad and your iPhone, you (or your partner) will be able to add new tasks in your iPhone app and within a couple of minutes they will be automatically added to your tasks list that is on your iPad. To do this, go to Settings and tap on the iCloud section and then ensure that you have entered the same account details on both devices. Now ensure that the 'Reminders' slider is switched to 'On' in the app list and you'll be good to go.

If you are using Reminders on the iPhone then it is also location-based, so you can set the app to remind you to pick up groceries, for example, as soon as you get close to a supermarket.

Just ensure that you have 'Location Services' turned on in Settings and that Maps is enabled and then you tap on a task in Reminders, select 'Show More…', tick 'Reminders' under 'iCloud' and then tap the 'Remind Me' option and turn on the 'At a Location' slider.

Key features
How you can ensure that your daily tasks are fulfilled

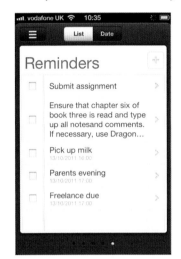

◀ Make lists
Reminders is laid out like a page in a notebook and whenever you wish to add something that you need to remember, you can tap a line on the page (or the '+' icon on the top bar) and you can then type a brief summary. It's a simple and intuitive system that allows you to keep track of important events and tasks that you need to complete and you can add as many as you need.

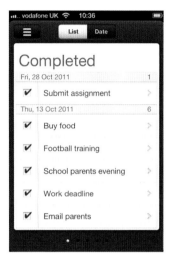

◀ Tick them off
Once you have successfully completed a task on your list, you can place a tick in the box next to the task to show that you have completed it. This allows you to keep track of what you have done and what you still have left to do on your 'To Do' list and any tasks that you have ticked as complete will be automatically added to the 'Completed' section. It's a good motivational tool as you'll find that you'll be spurred on as those ticks rack up.

"Keep track of what is left to do"

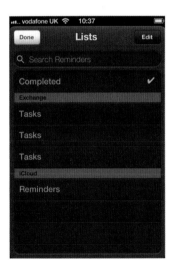

◀ Edit your lists
By default, your lists are organised into 'Reminders' (tasks still active) and 'Completed' (the tasks you have ticked off), which you can toggle between on the left-hand side of the screen. However, by tapping the 'Edit' button in the top-right corner you can create new lists, which is handy if you need to separate tasks into those that relate to work and your social life.

▶ Set reminders
If you need to remember to complete tasks on your list for a certain time or date then you can program in reminders by selecting a task to call up a box of options. Next tap on the 'Remind Me' section moving the 'On a Day' slider to 'On' and then tapping the date entry to determine a specific date and time. You will then be sent alerts which will flash up on your phone's screen at the designated time you set to remind you to complete the task.

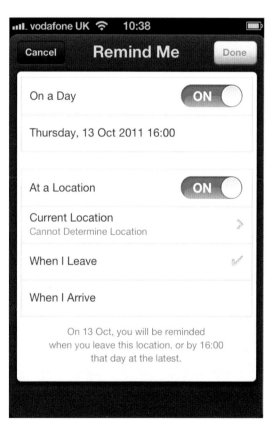

▲ Location reminders
If you need to pick up some groceries you can set a reminder so that the app notifies you as soon as you get within spitting distance of a supermarket. You'll never have a valid excuse for not picking up bread again.

Brainstorm on the move with Notes

Get the most out of the iPhone's note-taking app

Notes is a simple application that is all-too-often overlooked in favour of one of the many organiser tools on the App Store. But Notes is an invaluable resource. Its premise is simple, working on the concept of a journal, with blank pages ready to be filled with your thoughts.

In portrait orientation, you are presented with a full-screen blank page, perfect for when you want to write away without distractions. To browse through all your notes, you can use the previous and next arrows at the bottom of the screen, or hit the Notes menu. You can also delete notes, as well as email them directly.

In landscape, the application is perfect for heavy notetakers, as it gives you a bigger keyboard to type with, to ensure that you don't hit the wrong key as your fingers work overtime to catch up with your train of thought. Notes is an intuitive app that loads almost instantaneously, and is perfect for capturing any thoughts or ideas that pop into your head.

> "Notes is an invaluable resource, with blank pages ready to be filled with your thoughts"

● **List**
Tap here to go back to a list of your notes, with the current one highlighted

● **New note**
Hit the '+' icon in the top-right of the screen to open a new, blank note

● **Data detectors**
Phone numbers and addresses can be viewed instantly in Maps or Contacts

● **Trash**
Tap here to delete your note. It will then take you to the next note on your list

● **Share**
Use this envelope icon to email your note to yourself or others

---

Make the most of Notes' compatibility
Tailor your notes to work with other built-in iPhone apps

One of the best things about all iPhone apps is the fact that all of the built-in programs are designed to work with each other seamlessly. Notes is certainly no exception to this rule. Therefore, it pays to ensure that when you are creating new notes, you include information that can be picked up by the other apps.

If you list a name, you can instantly access that person's details via Contacts with a quick tap, so make sure that you list the full name of a person as listed in your contacts. Similarly, addresses can be viewed in Maps, so include full addresses that make it easier for the app to search accurate data. URLs will automatically become links so that you can view them with a tap in Safari.

To get the real power out of Notes, make sure that these sorts of details are included, and you will thank yourself for the effort when you go back and view notes at a later date.

Key features

Stay organised on the move with Notes

◀ New note

You can create a new note in either orientation by simply hitting the '+' sign in the top right-hand corner of the screen. This presents you with a new blank, lined page, which is date-stamped so that you can easily find it again. The note is titled by your first sentence or first few words, so it's best to always put a header that will make it easy to locate at a glance in the future.

◀ Email your thoughts

Another example of the compatibility between your iPhone's built-in apps is the way that you can email your notes directly from the icon at the bottom of each note. This places your note text as the main body of an email, with the subject line the same as the header. Feel free to edit it before sending.

"Notes works with other apps seamlessly"

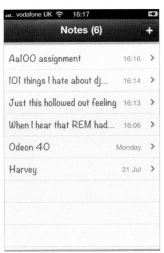

▶ Search notes

If you are prone to having a lot of notes on your iPhone, then it is essential that you can find the one that you need easily. In this case, you use the search field at the top of the note list. Here you can search for anything, such as name, date and keywords, to see all of the notes that match your search criteria anywhere within their content and save you the time spent flicking through them all.

◀ Note list

A list of all your notes can be accessed by tapping the 'Notes' button in the top left-hand corner of the screen. Your notes are listed in order of when they were created or modified. If you create multiple notes one after another, the time is listed on that day too. Tap a note header to open it and cycle through them by tapping the arrows at the bottom of the page.

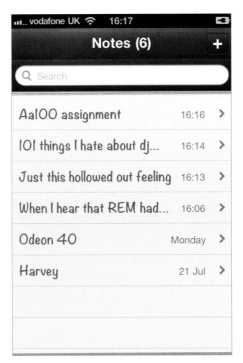

▲ Settings

There isn't a great deal that you can customise, but if you take a trip to the Settings menu you can pick one of three fonts. The default is Noteworthy, but you can go for the more classic Helvetica or the charming Marker Felt as well.

Make the most of Maps

This great app should end all those arguments of the best way to reach your destination

Gone are the days of having to carry an A-Z around with you – your iPhone does the same job, but better. If you are in an unfamiliar town or city looking for an office block for a business meeting, a hotel or just want to find nearby restaurant, with your iPhone you can quickly find where you are on a map and figure out how to reach your destination.

Your Maps app will cleverly pinpoint your location accurately using a combination of GPS, Wi-Fi and cellular towers and, as you move, your iPhone will update your location automatically. What's more, when you arrive you can drop a pin into your destination on a map and then share your location with others via iMessage, email or MMS and, if you're using iOS 5 you will even be able to tweet your location without leaving the Maps app – the perfect way for you to meet up with a group of friends. How did you ever live without it?

> "Gone are the days of having to carry an A-Z around with you"

Search
The Search screen has a search window in the top right to input location details

Bookmarks
The bookmarks icon gives you a list of bookmarked, recent or Contacts locations

Directions
Switch to the Directions screen to enter start and end points of a journey

Compass
This compass arrow, bottom left, can be pressed to find your current location

Menu
The menu options are found by turning the bottom right of the map over

QUICK TIP

Use different map views
Get detailed location information

The map can be viewed in three different ways, all of which can be accessed by tapping the curled page icon. The first, Standard, is the default setting, and this is the one that you will use the majority of the time, as it's best for navigating without any distractions. Satellite is perfect for pinpointing a certain building on a road, for example, as this gives you a photographic view of the area. It provides endless fun checking out your home address, but is also a practical feature as it can give you an insight as to the layout of a certain area and can help you find routes from, say, the carpark to the cinema. The third and final option is Hybrid, which is the same as the Satellite view, but with road markings from the Standard view over the top, allowing you to navigate easily, with the ability to zoom in and look in more detail when you get close. You'll likely find that you'll leave the map in Standard mode and never really use the other options, but it is worth experimenting to find the best view for each task you need to undertake.

Key features
Inside the Maps app

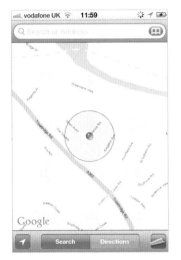

◀ Locate yourself
At the bottom of the map screen, there are various icons that are present. The compass arrow can be used to accurately locate yourself through your iPhone. Tap on it once, and a pin will appear at your present location, which can then be used to get directions to another place. Or, if you're a bit lost, getting the 'You are here' location can be invaluable. You will need an internet connection to use this feature.

◀ Get directions
By hitting Directions and choosing a start and end point, you can get accurate travel plans to go from one point to the other. By default, these will be driving directions, but you can choose to switch to walking instead. There is also an option to reveal public transport solutions, but this won't always be available in every area. With iOS 5 you can get multiple routes, so pick one and hit Start to get your directions.

"In iOS 5 you get multiple routes"

◀ Find places
To help you find places more easily, you have the Search box at the top of the screen. Start typing here, and your iPhone will begin looking for possible matches. It keeps a history of your Recent Searches, so any matches from what you type in will be automatically listed. You can list a town, road name, full address or point of interest, and if it's in the database, then you'll find it.

▶ Add bookmarks
You can easily bookmark locations so that you can find the same place in the future. It is worth bookmarking all your common locations, such as home, work and the gym. That way, it is easy to get directions from one point to another. To add a bookmark, tap the arrow next to the location and tap 'Add to Bookmarks'. You can also drop a pin to find your way back to a location – navigate to the area, then tap the curled page icon to reveal the hidden menu underneath, where you can select 'Drop Pin'.

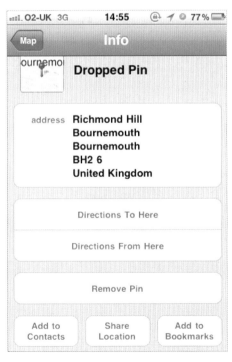

▲ Menu options
The map rolls up from the bottom right-hand corner to reveal a selection of options, including map views, placing pins and having a Traffic Overlay added so that you can avoid congestion in busy areas.

Use FaceTime to make video calls over Wi-Fi

Chat face to face in real time with anyone on a Mac, iPhone, iPod touch or iPad 2 with FaceTime enabled

 There must be very few people in the technological world who haven't heard or used Skype to make video calls over the internet with friends, family and colleagues. However, despite how amazing it is to see someone on the other side of the world (or town) and chat to them in a conversation on your computer screen, setting up an account to be able to use the service in the first place is something of a chore – especially when you have to find a username which no one has thought of yet.

This is where Apple's FaceTime comes into its own, allowing you to make calls wherever you may be. You can use either someone's iPhone number or their email address and you're good to go – no setup is necessary. As long as the person's online or by their phone, your call will get through. It finally takes the geekiness out of video calls and brings them into the hands of regular users.

> "Use either someone's iPhone number or their email address and you're good to go"

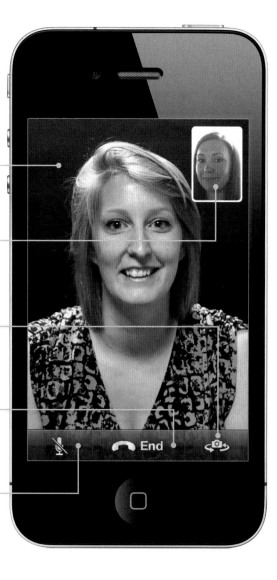

No 3G
Currently, FaceTime only works over Wi-Fi, not the 3G mobile network

You!
This little window of yourself can be moved around to any corner of the screen

Swap
Tap this button to switch to the rear camera and back again, if you need to use it

End button
Terminating the FaceTime call is a simple matter of tapping on this button

Mute button
This stops you from being heard. Tap on it again to reactivate the microphone

---

Use multiple accounts
When more than one person needs to use FaceTime from the same device

Once you've entered your Apple ID and chosen your preferred email address to be contacted through, FaceTime will run without any more setup on your part. But what if you share your iPhone with other people who would rather communicate using their own FaceTime username and password?

There doesn't appear to be any way to log out and sign in with another ID from the Phone app itself. This is because the app's main preferences reside elsewhere – in the Settings application, to be exact. Select it and scroll down to the bottom of the default options – beneath them is a section which contains the preferences for all of the main default apps that are pre-installed on your iPhone.

You'll find the FaceTime settings sandwiched between the Phone and Safari setting options, identified by the camera icon. From here it is possible to switch FaceTime off, add other email addresses that you can be contacted through and see which account is currently being used. Tap on that account's name in order to bring up a floating window that you can then use to sign out. Once you've done this, you can then log in using a different account, allowing more than one user.

Key features
Use your iPhone to see your friends and family

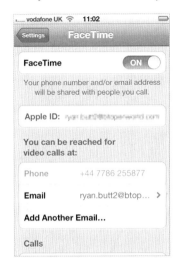

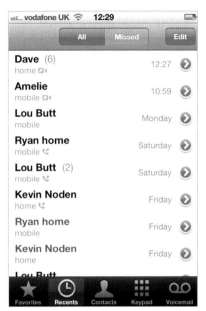

◀ Free calls
FaceTime is a service that is only available over Wi-Fi, but what that means is that it's a totally free service that you can use between certain iOS devices (iPhone 4 and 4S, iPad 2 and iPod touch) and Macs. All you need to do to start making FaceTime calls between devices is to go to Settings on your iPhone, turn FaceTime on (it has its own section) and ensure that you have a phone number and email address assigned.

◀ Recent calls
If you tap the 'Recents' tab in your Phone app, you'll be able to see everyone you've called recently, both regular talking calls and FaceTime calls – which are identifiable by the video camera icon that is under the person's name. Using this menu, along with the 'Favourites' tab is a good way to speed-up the calling process. If you know you want to chat to someone you called recently just tap the arrow next to the person's name to start a new FaceTime call. It's a quick and easy process.

◀ Organising Favourites
Adding people to your Favourites list is done either via their contact details or by tapping on the '+' button at the top-right of the screen while in the 'Contacts' tab. When you add a new person to your favourites you will be given the option of adding their details as either a 'Voice Call' or 'FaceTime', making it easy to pick out the people to talk face to face with.

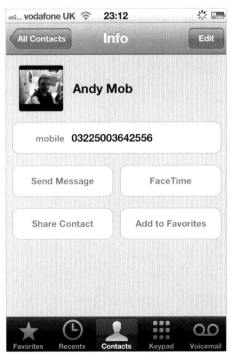

▶ Making calls
There are two different ways to initiate FaceTime calls through your iPhone. You can either launch your Phone app, choose the recipient you wish to call from the 'Contacts' tab and then tap 'FaceTime' or you can launch your Contacts app and start a visual chat from there using the same method. If the person you are calling is available and online you will see a video camera icon next to the 'FaceTime' option indicating that you are good to go. Once initiated, your camera conversation should soon start.

▲ Use the back camera
You don't just have to use the forward-facing camera to make video calls; you can take advantage of the back camera to show people what you can see around you. This can have many advantages, such as showing someone the location you're in, filming someone else who may be with you and much more. It opens up the flexibility of your video calling and is a great way of showing your caller more than just a headshot.

Get the most out of the Music app

Be one of the first to hear a new album wherever you are and access your tunes on the go

Chances are you have a portable music player already, so why would you want to turn your iPhone into one? Easy, it saves space in your pockets and allows you to ferry your music library around with you so it is on hand at all times for when you need it most. Thanks to the iOS 5 update, you can also enjoy many more features from your Music app (formerly known as your iPod app). Perhaps the most significant is the way in which you can sync your iTunes account to your iCloud, meaning that any songs you have purchased are pushed to all of your iOS devices wirelessly with no need to connect to you computer. But you can also browse the iTunes Store from your handset and buy new tracks and enjoy some great features while you play them. All of the best features of this great app are explained right here.

"Any songs you have purchased will be pushed to all of your iOS devices"

● Search
If you scroll down you will reveal a handy search function at the top

● Now Playing
View the playlist and contents of what's playing by tapping this icon

● Songs
Songs are listed alphabetically by song title in the main window

● Tabs
The tabs along the bottom offer different ways of viewing content

● More
The More tab holds elements such as podcasts, audiobooks and iTunes U

QUICK TIP

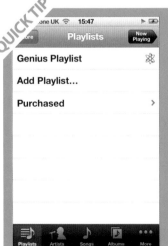

Utilise Genius music selections
Let your iPhone do the hard work of finding tunes you'll love

Genius is an Apple feature that you will find on all the latest iDevices, as well as the newest versions of iTunes on your Mac or PC. When you're listening to music and you come across a song that you really like, then you can hit the Genius button. The iPhone then goes through the tunes that you have on your device and creates a custom playlist of songs that it believes will go well together.

You can then choose to play the Genius playlist and save it for future listening, or start over again with another song that you love. Genius is the perfect alternative to a simple shuffle as you can tailor the sort of songs that come up to suit your mood, depending on the type of track initially chosen.

You may already have seen Genius pop up on some of your other devices, as it is

also available when browsing for new songs on iTunes, by recommending bands and albums that you might like to download, based on the sort of songs that you already own.

The App Store has a Genius category on the iPhone too, which works in much the same way. It recommends apps that you might want based on those you have previously bought and downloaded to your device.

Key features
Get the most out of the Music app

◀ Full-screen images
When you are listening to your tracks, you can view the album cover full screen. There is an info bar at the top with which you can see the artist, album and song title, as well as repeat and shuffle tracks. However, this can be hidden with a tap of the screen, so you can enjoy your artwork uncovered. A great display for when using the iPhone as a music player around the house.

◀ Album info
During playback in the full-screen mode, you can choose to see album listing information by hitting the menu icon in the top-right of the screen. This enables you to see what songs you have coming up next. You can hit any track to start a new song if you see something you fancy hearing sooner. The arrow takes you back to the playlist again.

"You can also sync music wirelessly from your iPad"

◀ Purchase from iTunes
You can buy audiobooks, podcasts, music, films and TV shows from the iTunes Store, which you can link to directly from within the Music app interface. Simply browse until you find something you like, hit the 'Buy' button and wait for it to download. You can also sync music and other files wirelessly from your computer or iPad via iCloud.

▶ Playlists
Creating your own custom playlist is the best way to hear the tunes that you want, whatever the occasion. Whether it's Christmas tunes to bring festive cheer, or cheesy Eighties pop for a house party, tap the 'Playlist' tab at the bottom of the screen and then hit 'Add Playlist…' to create a brand new playlist. Here you can give it a title to help you remember what's on it, then start populating it by choosing the tracks you want to include from the library listing that comes up automatically.

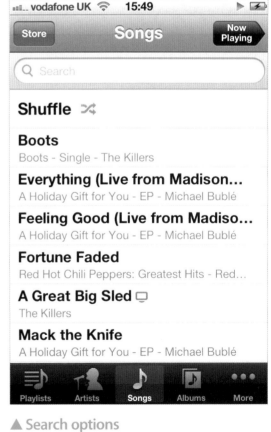

▲ Search options
There is a Search bar at the top of the screen (scroll down to reveal it), which is great if you know exactly what you want. The iPhone will start filtering content as you type to find you a match.

Master the Camera

How to use your versatile iPhone Camera to capture those unmissable and beautiful moments

The iPhone is an ideal device for capturing quick snaps and video as it's likely to always be on you and it is easy to share your images from within the app. The new iPhone 4S features an 8 megapixel camera (that's 60 per cent more pixels than the camera on the standard iPhone 4) and is engineered with a higher, full-well capacity to collect more light – making the images that you capture more detailed and better defined. And, with iOS 5 installed, you can share your images without leaving the Camera app, both by the usual channels such as email and text message, and via Twitter, which becomes integrated into all of your key apps.

You can also review the images you have captured by tapping the Camera Roll icon that's located in the bottom-left corner of the screen and make quick edits to your videos and images to save space. So it's time to ditch your dedicated digital camera and use your trusty iPhone for all your quick snapping needs.

"You can share your images without leaving the app"

● **Camera**
To swap from the rear to the front camera and back again, tap on this icon

● **Preview**
The entire iPhone screen offers you a giant preview of what you're shooting

● **Record**
When you're making a video, this record button pulsates from red to dark red

● **Browse**
All the photos you've taken can be browsed by tapping on this button

● **Slider**
You can take a photo or shoot a video. Make your choice by moving this slider

272 of 283

Trimming your clips
Basic editing is but a tap away

Recording video is far from an easy process, and more often than not you can end up with parts you don't need, especially at the start and end of your recording. Considering the fact that storage on your iPhone is somewhat limited, and how space-hungry HD video can be, it's a good idea to get rid of those unwanted sections. Thankfully, you don't need to have access to a video editing program

like iMovie to do this: you can perform this action straight from the Camera app itself.

Once you've finish taking your video, go to the Camera Roll and select the shot you wish to work with. You'll notice that as the clip plays out, a small playhead moves at the top of your screen over thumbnails of your video. Either side of this row of thumbnails are handles. Drag one inwards to turn them yellow, and start

the trimming process. You can drag either handle as often as you want until you're happy with your selection. Once done, tap on the yellow Trim button on the top right. You can then choose to delete the unwanted parts or save your selection as a new clip.

Trim Original

Save as New Clip

Cancel

Key features

The essential functions of the Camera app

◀ Two cameras, one device

If this is the first time that you have launched this application, then the back camera will be switched on by default, effectively letting you use the entire screen as a giant viewfinder. If you'd rather take a picture using the front camera (bear in mind though that it's of a much lower resolution than the back one), then all you have to do is tap on the switch icon, which is located on the top-right of your iPhone's screen.

◀ Stills and motion

Both the front and back cameras are capable of recording stills and videos. You can switch over to the other one by swiping the icon on the right of the screen. Aside from this icon, there aren't any visible signs to tell you which mode the app's in aside from a timer that appears once recording has started. To take quick photos in iOS 5, you can now use your volume up button on the side of your device to merrily snap away.

"The back camera is on by default"

◀ Camera Roll

Once you've taken a photo or recorded a scene, it's immediately saved to your Camera Roll – a section of the Photos app where all images taken with your iPhone are stored. To get to it, tap on the icon, lower left of the screen. When a shot's taken, you'll see it shrink and travel to that icon. You can browse through them, and even focus your search solely on either Photos or Videos.

▶ Orientation-aware

Your iPhone uses its accelerometer to determine which way is up. In your Camera app, it is used to ensure that your photos are saved in the correct orientation. When filming, though, you need to make sure the correct orientation is set prior to tapping on the record button. However, once the iPhone's started recording, it won't change orientation even if you physically rotate the device. If you're not careful, you could end up inadvertently recording a scene sideways because of this.

▲ Roll options

You can share your images directly from the Camera Roll. Tap on the share icon (a rectangle with an curved arrow) in the bottom left of the screen. This brings up a series of options to share your images.

Explore the Photos app

It's here that all your videos and photos are stored, but this app is more than just a digital album

If you've got a Mac, you're undoubtedly using the iPhoto application as a place to store and catalogue your digital photos. The Photos application serves this very same purpose on the iPhone and from within the app it is possible to carry out some very simple edits, review, catalogue and even share your images without having to plug your device into your computer, and it's all thanks to iOS 5.

Whenever you take photos or capture video on your iPhone, they will automatically be stored in your Photos app and listed in a Camera Roll by the date that they were taken. By tapping on your Camera Roll you can then sort your images by tapping the share button on the thumbnail screen, highlighting your images and then choosing to delete them, add them to new or existing albums (that you can create in-app) or share them via email, multimedia message (MMS) or Tweet. You can also get all of the images captured on your iPhone pushed to all of your other devices via iCloud. Read on to find out more…

"You can edit, review, catalogue and share your images within the app"

● **Back**
To go back to your album (or all of your photos), simply tap on this button

● **Scrub**
You can scrub through your video by dragging this thick playhead

● **Play**
If you can't use the Play button on the clip, you can use this one instead

● **Share**
You can send your clip directly to YouTube from the Share menu

● **Trash**
You can instantly delete any unwanted images by tapping the wastebin here

---

Create a slideshow
Choose an album and enjoy the show

Your iPhone can make a great picture frame. It's such an obvious part of the design that there's even a slideshow option right on your Lock Screen.

However, this feature draws from your entire library of images by default which may not suit your purposes. If you want to be more selective, choose an album from the Photos application and bring it up full screen. You should now notice that a play button

appears on the bottom bar. Tap this and you will open up a page of Slideshow options.

Here you can set the Transitions (the animation that fades one image into another) and determine whether your device plays music to accompany your slideshow and, if so, what. To pick appropriate music, tap the 'Music' option and then pick a track from your Music app library. When you're ready, tap on 'Start

Slideshow' and enjoy the show. You can get out of your slideshow at any time by tapping on the screen or by swiping left or right to go to the previous or next image on the list.

Transitions	Cube >
Play Music	ON
Music	¡Happy Birthday Guadal… >
Start Slideshow	

Key features
Exploring your Photos app

◀ Create albums
With previous operating systems, if you wanted to create new albums in which to store photos on your iPhone you had to do so via iTunes; with iOS 5 you can do it from your device. On your Albums page, tap 'Edit' and then 'Add'. You will then be able to name your new album, after which it will be added to your list. In order to add images to your albums, open your Camera Roll then tap the 'Share' button, highlight your chosen image and then tap 'Add To' and pick a destination.

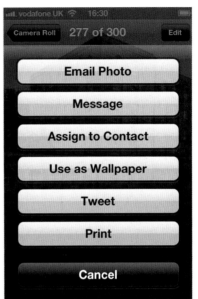

◀ Share photos
You'll find the Share menu acts differently depending on which part of the interface you find yourself in. When you see multiple thumbnails, it is possible to select more than one to email, copy, print or delete. However, focus on a single image and you can assign it to a contact's profile (and the image will pop up each time they call), use it as a wallpaper background for your phone and even Tweet about it, which we discuss in more detail below.

◀ Use the Photo Stream
One of the new additions to the Photo app that comes as part of the iOS 5 update is Photo Stream. This feature works with iCloud to push all of your images and videos to all of your iOS devices. What it means in practice is that you will be able to take photos on your iPhone and they will automatically appear in Photo Stream on your iPad. Even if you transfer photos from a digital camera onto your computer, copies will go to your devices.

▶ Tweet your photos
New to iOS 5 is the brilliant, time-saving Twitter integration for all of the key apps, including Safari, YouTube, Maps, Camera and, of course, Photos. If you wish to tweet about an image you have taken that's residing on your Camera Roll, open up the image in question and then tap the Share button. Among the list of options will be a button that says 'Tweet'. Tap this and your image will be attached to a text box. Write in the message that you want and then press 'Send' to share it with the world.

▶ Zoom in
Tap on a photo for it to zoom in and fill the screen (if you see black borders on either side of it, rotate your iPhone to change its orientation). You can also zoom into your photo to see greater detail – just place two fingers on the screen and move them away from each other. Bring them closer to zoom out. This also works with video clips stored in your photo library.

Use the YouTube app

The built-in YouTube app offers all the features of the website on your computer, in the palm of your hand

Odds are that you've visited YouTube in the last few weeks to see the latest viral video. The YouTube app included with your iPhone allows you to watch videos full screen and in HD when available. The app takes advantage of the touch screen technology, allowing you to view and control videos with a few taps, just like you would for movies stored on your phone. You can view videos in widescreen mode by turning your iPhone on its side, and it allows you to easily browse featured, related, most viewed, and top rated videos. You can also use the search feature to locate videos by keyword. What's more, you can log in with your YouTube account and bookmark your favourites. While logged in, you can also comment on and rate videos. The app remembers your viewing history, so you can locate videos you've recently watched to see them again.

"The YouTube app allows you to watch videos full screen and in HD when available"

History
This keeps track of videos you've viewed. You can tap 'Clear' to remove your history

My Videos
Videos you have uploaded to YouTube under your current username appear when you tap 'My Videos' while logged in

Subscriptions
Subscriptions displays videos of authors whose streams you have subscribed to

Most Viewed
To see the most popular videos ever, tap on the 'Most Viewed' category at the bottom of the page

Featured
Tap on 'Featured' to view a list of the current popular videos that have recently been uploaded

QUICK TIP

Subscribe to videos
Keep track of your favourite video creators

Say you really like a band's wacky music videos, and you watch them again and again. You want to keep track of the current videos and know when new ones are added.

The YouTube app lets you stay on top of everything an author has published to YouTube using Subscriptions. To add a subscription, view one of the videos by the author in small screen view. Tap on the 'More

Videos' button. At the top of the list, tap the 'Subscribe' button. You can now view your new subscription by tapping the 'More' button on the bottom of the screen and then choosing 'Subscriptions'. The Subscriptions screen shows you a list of your current subscriptions. Tap on each to see all videos currently on YouTube for that author, ordered from most recent to oldest. As new videos from these

authors are added, they will then automatically appear in your lists.

There are two ways to unsubscribe. From the Subscriptions screen, tap the 'Edit' button, and then tap the name of the subscription you want to delete, then tap 'Done'. To unsubscribe in small screen mode, view one of the videos from the author. Tap on 'More From', and then tap the 'Unsubscribe' button.

Key features
Finding your way around the YouTube app

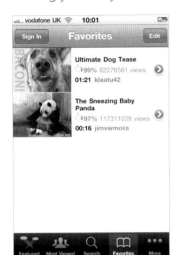

◀ Add Favourites
When viewing a video in the full screen mode (landscape), tap on the bookmark button to the left of the controls to save the current video as a favourite; the movie you selected will then be added to the 'Favourites' section of the options at the bottom of the main YouTube window. You can tap the 'Edit' button to remove saved favourites from your list.

◀ Share
When viewing a video in full screen mode, tap the share button to the right of the controls (the one that resembles an envelope) to send the current video to people you know. Tapping this button will instantly bring up an email window, which includes the name of the video in the subject header, and the message window will contain a link to the clip and a 'Check out this video…' message.

"Stay on top of your favourites"

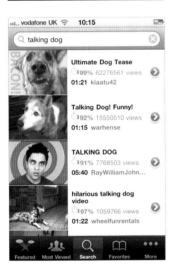

◀ Search
If you want to search for a particular video then tap on the 'Search' button contained in the list of options at the bottom of the screen. A search field will then be displayed at the top of the screen, and you will be able to enter keywords to help you find what you are looking for. Enter words and then tap 'Search', and all relevant videos will be displayed under the search field.

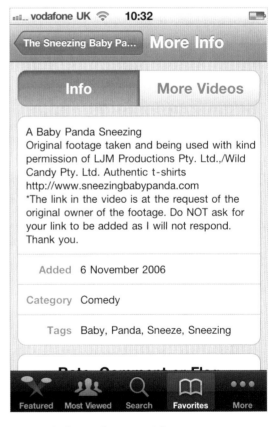

▶ View full screen
You can view full screen videos by turning your iPhone on its side. Tap the video you wish to view, and if it's still in small screen mode, tap the expand icon on the top right of the small video display, which looks like two tiny outward-pointing diagonal arrows. When in full screen mode, return to small screen by tapping the contract icon, which is a reversed version of the expand icon: two inward-pointing arrows in the top-right corner of the screen.

▲ Get info and more videos
After viewing a video, tap 'Done' and you'll be taken to a page about it. Tap 'Info' to get information and comments, or to rate, add comments or flag the video. Tap 'More Videos' to see more from the same user.

Play with Game Center

Learn how to play games and get competitive with your friends on Apple's Game Center

Game Center is the app that lets you keep track of the games you've played, the games your friends have played and how you stack up against them. It even enables you to compete against people you don't know in multiplayer games.

You can use Game Center to invite friends using their nickname or email address, and once you're connected you can see what games your competitive buddies are playing, their current status, and how they're doing.

To set yourself off on the path to gaming glory, open the Game Center app and sign in with your Apple ID. You will only have to do this once, because once you log in, you will stay logged in to the app until you choose to log out. You can type in a status message that will be visible to friends once you've made contact with them, or you can begin playing by clicking on the Games link and choosing one of your installed Game Center-compatible games. Game Center will keep track of your high scores and achievements and display them on your friends' Game Center.

"You can see what games your friends are playing and how they're doing"

Status
Type a current status in this box to share it with your friends

Games
Tap to open the Games screen with links to the games you've purchased

Friends
See all your current friends and the games that they're playing

Account
Tapping the Account banner opens your Game Center settings

Requests
View your pending friend requests when you tap on the Requests button

Find games
Getting around the Game Center App Store

When you're on the Games screen, tap the Find Game Center Games banner. This opens the Game Center App Store. On this screen, you'll see a sample of the most popular Game Center games. All the games in this store are Game Center-compatible games and will appear in the Game Center when you purchase them.

You will be presented with a list of different categories, which is a good place to start searching for new games, so tap on a category and then you will be given a list of games. From this screen you can explore the most popular games (and download what everyone else is playing) and find out the latest releases.

You can purchase a game by tapping on the button to the right of the game back on the main Game Center App Store screen. When you click on a game, you see a detailed screen with a button to purchase it, a description, user reviews, and other useful links. To quickly get back to the main Game Center App Store screen, tap the Game Center button on the upper left corner of the screen.

Key features

Getting to know the parts of Game Center

◄ Me

This is the main page you will see of the Game Center app – this is like your base home screen. From here you can set your status and photo, jump to the various other categories via the tabs at the bottom of the screen and view your current Game Center score, which is determined by the number of achievements that you have accumulated on the various Games Center compatible games that are installed on your device.

◄ Friends

The Friends screen displays all your Game Center friends. Tapping on each person's name in the list opens his or her details. You see how many friends they have and how many different games they have played. Drag down on the list to get a search box that lets you search for friends and you will also be provided with a selection of friend 'Recommendations', which can consist of friends of friends, or just people who play the same kind of games as you do. With Games Center you can build up your own gaming network.

◄ Games

Tap the Games tab to open the Games screen. Here you see the Game Center games you have installed. Tap on each game to get your current score, number of achievements and your rank. While on a specific game screen, you can also tap the 'Play' button to launch it. Like Friends, you will be provided with a selection of 'Game Recommendations' based on your interests.

► Friend requests

Send a request to a friend with Game Center by using the Requests tab. On this screen, tap 'Add Friends' and then enter a person's email address or Game Center nickname, if you know it. When you have entered all of the details and a message (it's bad manners to send a blank friend request, you know), tap 'Send' and wait for the recipient to respond to your request. You can also send friend requests from within the 'Friends' tab using Friend Recommendations, if you prefer.

▲ Account settings

To get to your Game Center account settings, tap on the Me button. Tap the yellow banner that says Account, followed by your email address. Tap on View Account. Use this screen to control whether you allow other people to send you invites, choose if other users can find you by using your email account and add another email so you can be found with that as well.

Use iBooks to read on your iPhone

Download and read eBooks and get involved in the digital revolution

The iBooks app is Apple's answer to the Kindle. You can purchase and download books from the iBookstore, then view and organise your titles on your virtual bookshelf. Read your books and adjust screen brightness, font size, and font face for more readability. Search for words, characters or phrases anywhere in your books. Change page colour to white or sepia and change the text layout to left or fully justified. As you're reading, highlight text and add notes. The page navigator on the bottom of each page helps you keep track of where you are.

If you need to stop reading, create a bookmark so you can come back later. iBooks allows you to read ePub and PDF-formatted books and documents. In addition to purchasing books from the iBookstore, you can add PDF documents from the Mail app and both PDF and ePub documents by adding them to iTunes and syncing your iPhone.

"Purchase and download titles from the iBookstore, then view and organise your titles on your virtual bookshelf"

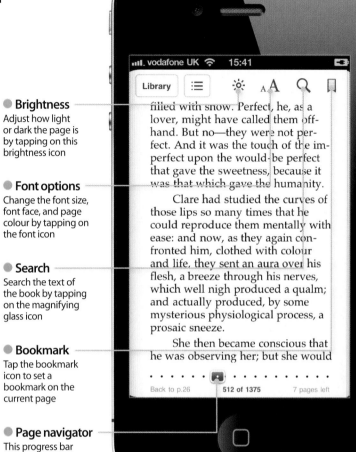

● Brightness
Adjust how light or dark the page is by tapping on this brightness icon

● Font options
Change the font size, font face, and page colour by tapping on the font icon

● Search
Search the text of the book by tapping on the magnifying glass icon

● Bookmark
Tap the bookmark icon to set a bookmark on the current page

● Page navigator
This progress bar shows you how far you are in the book

View book details in the iBookstore

Get more information on individual books in the iBookstore

When you locate a book in the iBookstore, tapping on it opens the detail screen. This screen is full of helpful tools and information, and it's available on every single book. On the top right is the link back to the previous page.

Just beneath it is the 'Alert Me' link. Whenever this author has a new publication, you'll receive an alert. You can also send an email to a friend with information on

this book. The basic information about the book is displayed to the right of the cover image, as well as a button to purchase the book. If you want to read a few pages of the book before buying, tap the 'Get Sample' button. A sample will be automatically added to your bookshelf.

If you scroll down the detail screen, you will see a graphical summary of customer ratings. Scroll further down to read any

customer reviews, and you can rate the book yourself by tapping on the star icons just under the 'Customer Ratings' section. Finally, you can see other, similar books that customers who bought this book also purchased. Tap on the cover of one of these to see its detail page. When you're done, tap the link to your previous page at the top, or hit 'Library' to return to your virtual bookshelf.

Key features
Functions that enhance your reading experience

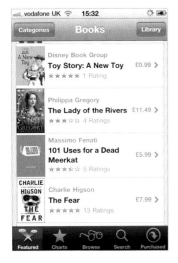

◀ Shop for books
The iBookstore is where you shop for books to add to your iBooks app. Open the store by tapping on the button on the upper left of your screen. Once there, you can view featured titles, search by title or author, and see bestsellers. Tapping an individual title gives you more information, including a description and customer reviews. Books you purchase are automatically transferred to your iBooks app and appear on your bookshelf.

◀ Organise your books
After you've used iBooks for a while, you'll have a number of books. To help you keep them organised, you can group them into collections. By default, you begin with two collections: Books and PDFs. Titles are automatically placed in the appropriate one. Tap the 'Collections' button on the upper right to see yours. You can add more, for example when grouping by genre. Tap the 'Edit' button and then the book you wish to move to a collection.

"Create collections to keep organised"

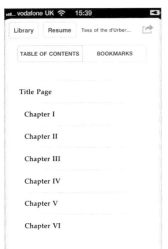

◀ View the table of contents
Each book includes a table of contents. It allows you to see at a glance the chapter titles and gives you a quick way to access chapters by tapping on the title. To get to the table of contents, tap a book to open it, and then tap on the button on the upper left, next to the 'Library' button. When you are done viewing the table of contents, tap the 'Resume' button.

▶ Search the bookshelf
You can search your bookshelf by title or author. In bookshelf view, the search box is normally hidden. To reveal it, drag down on the bookshelf. As you type, the books with titles or author names that match the search remain visible. It searches both first and last names and all words in the title, but not the contents of the books – you'll have to go into the books themselves to do that. To clear the results and display all of your titles, tap the small 'X' in the search box.

▲ Change the listing style
You can tap and hold on books to move them around and organise them. You can also view your titles in a list view by tapping the button with three horizontal lines, on the top left of your display next to the 'Edit' button.

Read magazines on your Newsstand

All of your favourite magazines are available in one handy place on the Newsstand app for iPhone

 One of the more eye-catching features of iOS 5 is Newsstand, an app not unlike iBooks that sits prominently on your Home screen. Like iBooks, Newsstand catalogues all of your magazines and newspapers in one place, lays them out on virtual shelves for easy access and updates them when new issues become available. There is also now a dedicated section in the App Store for all the essential reads, which you can access directly in-app and download new editions straight to your stand to enjoy whenever you want to kick back and relax. Using the app is a convenient way to keep up to date with your favourite digital publications and makes reading on your device even easier. So say goodbye to stacks of well-thumbed monthlies and enjoy your complete mag library in one handy place.

"Say goodbye to stacks of well-thumbed monthlies; with Newsstand you can enjoy your complete mag library in one handy place"

● **Tap and read**
When you tap on your Newsstand Home screen icon your virtual shelves will pop up on screen

● **Browse**
You can access the App Store from within the Newsstand app to make getting new issues a quick and easy process

● **Newsstand**
Issues of your favourite magazines and newspapers are laid out on shelves for clear organisation

● **Easy access**
Issues are downloaded straight into the app; gone are the days of separate apps for each individual magazine

● **Great reads**
Simply tap the cover of a magazine to open its respective app and start reading the latest issues

QUICK TIP

Find your favourites
How to discover and download great magazines from the App Store

We have already mentioned how easy it is to shop for new issues of your favourite magazines and how you can do it via the App Store or through the press of a button from within your Newsstand app, but it is good to know your way around the App Store to find what you are looking for.

When you tap on the 'Newsstand' category (or jump to it directly form your app),

the first page you see will be of featured magazines and staff favourites. This is a good place to start shopping as you can see what's popular. But if you tap on the 'Release Date' tab at the top of the page you will be treated to the complete catalogue of available magazines and newspapers, so you can browse through page by page to find what interests you. Alternatively, type the name of the magazine

you're looking for into the Search window to be taken straight to your selection.

Key features
Read all about it via your own virtual newsagent

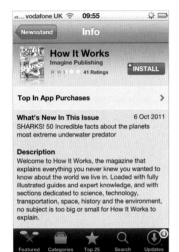

◀ Download your favourites
Purchasing and downloading new magazines and issues for your Newsstand is easy. You can browse all the new releases in a new dedicated section on the App Store and you can even obtain them from within the Newsstand app by tapping the 'Store' button in the top-right corner of the screen. All purchases will then be downloaded and stored on the virtual shelves – just launch the Newsstand app to access them.

◀ Delete issues
If you no longer want a particular magazine or newspaper displayed on the prestigious shelves of your Newsstand then deleting them is easy. You simply press and hold on a cover and the covers will begin to shake. When they do, tap the 'X' icon next to a particular cover and you will be asked if you would like to delete it from your Newsstand. Bear in mind though that new issues replace the old ones on your shelves, so don't delete things by mistake.

◀ Get new issue alerts
Keep a close eye on the Newsstand app icon on your Home screen because a red alert will notify you when new issues become available. You can also add individual magazines to your Notification Center, so you'll be made aware of the arrival of a new issue as soon as it hits the store. It certainly beats trudging down to your local newsagent to shop for the latest magazines and daily papers.

▶ Browse issues
You can easily browse your magazine collection by the well rendered covers that are laid out on your shelves. In order to read a magazine you simply tap on the cover of the one you want to open and the individual app for that publication will launch. The magazine apps you download are viewing portals only, so you will need to purchase individual issues through the respective apps. There is plenty of free stuff to enjoy though, such as complimentary issues given away with the apps to get you reading.

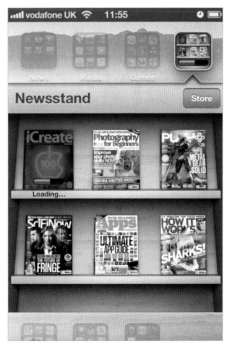

The New York Times

WHITE HOUSE MEMO
A Silver Lining to America's Waning Influence
President Obama will travel this week to the Group of 20 summit in France as the leader of a nation that no long...

NEWS ANALYSIS
Austerity Faces Test as Greeks Question Their Ties to Euro
The euro crisis has finally touched real politics, with the Greeks now questioning whether their commitment to...

DEALBOOK
Federal Inquiry of MF Global Escalates
Multiple federal agencies are examining whether the bankrupt brokerage firm run by Jon S. Corzine diverted customer money to support its own trades.

Drug Terms Reduced, Freeing Prisoners
More than 1,800 prisoners are eligible for release under

▲ Read with ease
Reading on your device is a liberating experience and a lot of digital magazines on the market embrace the technology to make the process a fully interactive experience, with much more to discover within the apps than words alone. Not only does Newsstand make it quick and convenient to buy the latest magazines, it also makes reading them a joy and far more practical than thumbing through the greasy pages of the physical formats.

Master Siri for iPhone 4S

The iPhone 4S's new voice control feature will help you totally reorganise your life and speed up tasks

There are a few good reasons to purchase the iPhone 4S, but none of them are quite as compelling as Siri, the personal assistant that is built into every new model of the iPhone. The new software will activate with a click and hold of the iPhone's Home button, bringing up the Siri assistant at the bottom of the screen. You can ask it questions or give it instructions, but what makes it truly impressive is the way in which it understands what it is you're asking in context. So, if you want to know whether or not you're going to need a coat in the morning, you don't need to ask about the weather; just ask whether you need a coat, and Siri will answer you, and show you the weather for good measure.

With a range of dialects and languages, and a system that learns how you speak the more you talk to it, this is the most advanced voice recognition system available on any consumer device right now.

> "This is the most advanced voice recognition system available on any consumer device right now"

● **What can you do?**
If you're not sure what Siri can do, simply ask it! Siri will show a list of what is possible

● **More options**
Tap one of the options on the list to find out the many ways to ask each question

● **Wi-Fi or 3G**
Siri needs the web to work, so unless you have 3G or Wi-Fi it won't work at all

● **Questionable**
Give an instruction that requires Siri to ask you a question and it will activate automatically without touching the button

● **Activation Button**
Once Siri is activated by holding the Home Button, you can tap this button to activate Siri

Have fun with Siri
It's not all work with the iPhone's assistant

While Siri is incredibly useful for scheduling meetings, making reminders, or sending messages when driving or running, it's certainly not a case of all work and no play. Apple has included its own charm into the software built into the iPhone 4S, giving it some interesting responses to certain questions. There are several funny reactions buried in the Siri interface, and they just take a little digging to find.

There are already whole websites dedicated to finding the funniest, quirkiest and most interesting responses that Siri can come up with, but it's worth trying some out for yourself as you never know what Easter eggs you may come across while playing around. For some, there are even a number of responses, so you can say a sentence like "Beam me up, Scotty" a number of times and hear a different

reaction each time. If you want, Siri will even tell you a story…

This is just one more reason why Siri has become such a sensation among iPhone users so quickly – it appears to have personality. Obviously this is programmed by Apple, but where other phones require you to speak in a certain way to activate features, Siri appears to be closer to human than anything before it.

Key features
Siri's top functions to help your day-to-day life

◀ Understanding context
Siri will understand a series of questions or commands based on what you asked before. You won't need to ask a full question repeatedly, so if you want to see what time it is in different cities, for example, you can just start your question with "What about…?" This is what makes Siri so incredible – you can talk to your phone like you would do to a real person, and it will understand what you mean.

◀ Reading messages
When you receive a text or an email, you can ask Siri to read it out loud to you. It will even understand and pronounce punctuation so you know exactly what everything says. When the message has been read, Siri will ask if you want to reply or hear it again, and replying is as simple as saying "tell her…" Siri will translate what you say into text and prepare it to send; this is great when you're driving and can't use your phone.

"Siri will turn what you say into text"

◀ Searching for information
If you ask a question that isn't something Siri can answer on its own, it will search through the online Knowledge Engine, Wolfram Alpha. It contains answers to thousands of questions, and may show you more information. This is perfect if you want to quickly check a fact, or if you just want to impress your friends with all kinds of interesting bits of information.

▶ Dictation
Because Siri is currently in the beta production stage, it can't yet write messages such as Tweets within the main Siri app. However, whenever a keyboard slides up from the bottom of the screen on the iPhone 4S you'll notice that there is new microphone button in the lower-left corner. Tap on the button, and you can begin to dictate messages, which Siri cleverly translates into words on the message screen. Tap 'Done' when you're finished, and your words will be typed out for you on screen.

▲ Mutual understanding
What makes Siri really powerful is that you can address it in a huge number of ways. While you can say obvious things like "set up a meeting tomorrow," you can ask questions or phrase instructions in many other forms.

Lifestyle

In-depth guides that will help enhance your day-to-day life

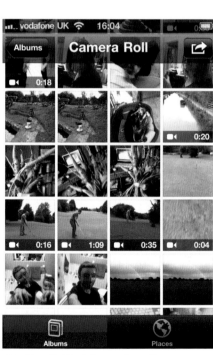

80 Edit videos directly on your iPhone

86 Use Facebook Chat+ to keep in touch with friends

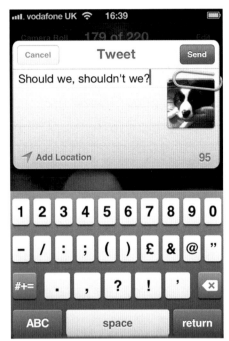

88 Master Twitter intregation on your phone

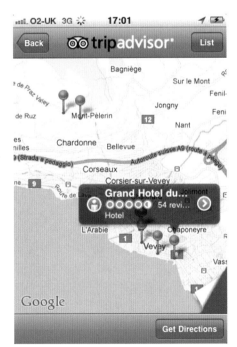

90 Plan your next holiday with the TripAdvisor app

92 Translate foreign text with ease thanks to Word Lens

"Allow your phone to make your life a whole lot easier"

Difficulty: Beginner **Time needed:** 5 minutes

Take faster photos

Use the abilities of the iPhone to take great photos much faster using the volume button

While the iPhone has been able to take photos since its original launch, the only technique to do so up until now has been a tap of the screen to take your snap. But due to the shape and layout of the iPhone, you may have found that it isn't always convenient to hold it steady in position with one hand and, then touch the capture button with the other, and you may have been seeking an alternative shooting method.

Thankfully, there is now a way around this minor gripe. The release of iOS 5 has brought with it several new abilities inside the Camera app, all of which make taking and viewing photos a lot quicker and easier. By far the most useful feature, though, is the option to take a snapshot with the 'Volume +' button on the side of your device. It's quick, easy, and most of all it's comfortable to reach when holding the iPhone up to take your photo, making this arguably one of the most useful new additions to iOS 5.

However, that isn't the end of it. Viewing your photos is even easier thanks to a new way to access your Camera Roll, and now you can even edit your photos on the iPhone as soon as you've taken them, ensuring that even a skewed shot can be straightened out right on your device. Now, there really is no excuse not to get snapping on your iPhone.

Camera | Take incredible photos

1: Know the screen
The Camera screen has a lower bar with the shutter button (but you can use the volume button in iOS 5). There are also buttons at the top to switch cameras and access settings.

2: Zoom in and out
In iOS 5, the gesture for zooming has changed. Rather than tapping to bring up the bar then sliding it along, you can pinch in and out with two fingers.

3: Video record
By tapping or swiping the toggle in the bottom right-hand corner of the screen, you can switch to your video camera and record 720p movies.

Taking a fast snapshot
Make the most of the Camera app

Volume button
Tapping the volume button on the top right of your iPhone will allow you to take a snap without even touching the screen

Swipe to your library
New in iOS 5 is the ability to access your Camera Roll without carefully tapping the icon in the bottom left. Simply swipe from the left edge

Tap to expose
You can tap anywhere on the screen to make a small focus square appear. It sets the focus on the item you tapped, and alters the lighting of the scene

Photo editing
In iOS 5, when you've taken a shot, you can edit the photo right there on your iPhone by choosing the Edit button when viewing your photos. This will give you options to enhance, straighten, crop and rotate your shot, as well as giving you the chance to remove red-eye.

Options
The iPhone 4S has an LED flash but with other models your options are limited to adding gridlines to the screen and turning on HDR

4: Turn on Gridlines
If you want to line up your shots perfectly, you can turn Gridlines on by tapping the Options button at the top of the screen, and then swiping the slider.

5: Face the front
The front-facing camera on the iPhone isn't just for FaceTime – it can also be used to take snapshots. Just tap the icon in the top right of the screen.

6: View your shots
If you tap in the bottom left of the screen on the tiny image, you'll view your camera roll, but in iOS 5 you can also swipe from the left edge of the screen.

Difficulty: Beginner   Time needed: 10 minutes

Edit images in Photos

Make the most of your iPhone camera, and take advantage of the new iOS 5 photo-editing feature

The introduction of iOS 5 has brought over 200 new features to the table. One of which is the ability for iPhone users to edit photos directly on the device using the aptly titled Photos app. Admittedly, the editing software isn't going to turn you into David Bailey or your photos into works of art, yet it does help to enhance both photos taken with the camera and photos already on the device.

The Editing features available include the ability to rotate images from portrait to landscape. There's also an enhance option, which can adjust the colour depth, brightness and contrast, thus transforming a

relatively dull photo into something that is altogether more pleasant to look at. The last few options should prove to be useful as well; the first of these allows you to remove the notorious red-eye that you get in photos which have been overloaded with flash, and the second enables you to crop images. Again, this helps when you only want a specific part of a photo, and want to remove the rest.

For this tutorial, you will have needed to upgrade your iPhone to the latest iOS 5 firmware, as not all of the features highlighted here are available with earlier operating systems. Simply connect your device to iTunes, and it will prompt the update automatically.

Photos | Edit your shots

1: Select your photo
Launch the Photos app from the home screen, then choose your Camera Roll or an album containing images, pick an image, and then tap 'Edit'.

2: Rotate the photo
From the Edit Photo screen, select the 'Rotate' option at the bottom, and keep tapping this in order to rotate the orientation. Tap 'Save' when you are done.

3: Enhance the image
If you choose 'Enhance', the software will adjust the colours of the image. Tap the same option again to cancel the changes, or tap 'Save' to finish.

Editing interface

Editing your photos is as intuitive as the iPhone itself

Multi-touch controls
Before you choose how to edit a photo, you can use the multi-touch pinch controls to zoom into the photo to focus on the areas you want to improve

Enhance
On the surface this seems like a basic option compared to most dedicated editing packages, but in practice it's a great feature that can transform your photo within moments

Undo any changes
Thanks to the intuitiveness of the iPhone, you can easily revert back to the original image by pressing cancel, and then quickly re-save it

Forward photo
Once you have made changes to your photo, you can use the share option (bottom left corner) to assign the photo to your Home or Lock screen, email, Tweet or even print it (if you have a compatible wireless printer attached). The 'Assign to Contact' menu choice is also useful for adding images next to your contacts' names.

Crop photos
Crop is another under-estimated feature. You can chop out parts of the photo (could be a blurred section) that you don't want any more

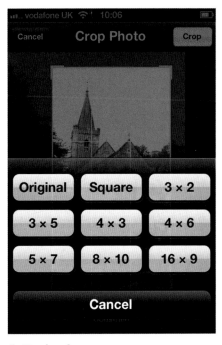

4: Remove red-eye
Select an image where people have red-eye, then tap on the 'Red-Eye' option. Next, click on the people's eyes to remove the red. Click 'Save' to finish.

5: Crop the photo
Select an image to edit, and from the list of options, choose 'Crop'. Drag your finger to re-size the photo, or alternatively, you can tap on 'Constrain'.

6: Undo changes
If you've made a mistake during the editing process, you can always choose the 'Cancel' command at the top of the screen to leave your images untouched.

Difficulty: Beginner **Time needed:** 5 minutes

Save from Photo Stream to your library

Save photos from Photo Stream to store in your personal album

 Photo Stream, which Apple introduced with iOS 5, is an innovative way to share your photos across your Apple devices. When it is switched on and you are on a wireless network, all new photos that you take with your iPhone will be uploaded to your iCloud account, provided of course that you have signed up for one (it you haven't, why not, it's free?!). The idea behind Photo Stream is that you don't have to manually upload the images or even choose which ones to upload, as they are all sent by default when you have a network connection. This has several advantages. For a start, the Photo Stream tab will appear across all your devices as well as in iPhoto or Aperture on your Mac if you are running OS X 10.7.2, so you can view all the pictures you have taken while out and about without having to do anything on those devices. Even better, imagine you have an iPhone and an iPad but when you go on holiday you just take your iPhone. While you are away, your flatmate uses your iPad and is able to see all of your pictures automatically because they have been uploaded to Photo Stream. It's a quick and easy way to share pictures, and it's also possible to save items from the stream to your device so that you have them with you at all times without worrying if you have access to your Photo Stream via a Wi-Fi network.

Photos | Save photos locally from Photo Stream

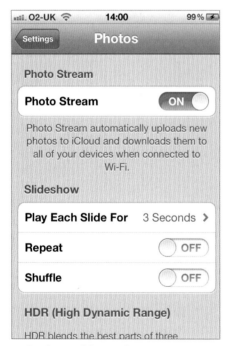

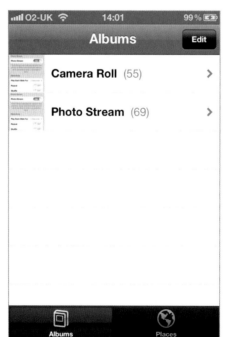

1: Activate Photo Stream
You'll need to have activated Photo Stream before taking pictures since it's only after this that pictures will be uploaded – it won't upload existing snaps.

2: View the pictures
Go into your Photos app and, as well as the Camera Roll, you should now see a Photo Stream section. Tap on this in order to see the uploaded pictures.

3: View by album or place
Tap on Photo Stream to access it. You can choose to view pictures by album or by places. Tap a location to see just the photos that were taken there.

Download your pictures from Photo Stream
Pull photos out of the cloud

Choosing images
Tap on a picture to select it and, in the next step, select what action to perform. Choose as many images as you like

Share
This button will allow you to share a number of photos over a text message or print them wirelessly if you are set up for it

Wireless connectivity
It's best to only use Photo Stream over a wireless connection unless you're lucky enough to have unlimited 3G data on your data plan. Uploading high-res pictures can use a lot of bandwidth and time, as well as sapping your battery, so go with Wi-Fi wherever possible.

Network activity
The spinning dial shows that your iPhone is in the process of sending pictures to or downloading them from Photo Stream in the cloud

Save
With images selected from Photo Stream, tap the Save button to save a copy locally onto your iPhone

4: Choose pictures
Go back to Photo Stream and click the arrow button at the top-right corner. Then tap each picture that you would like to download and click the Save button.

5: Check the results
Go back in to your Camera Roll and you will see that the images have downloaded. Be aware that this might take a minute or two if there are lots of images.

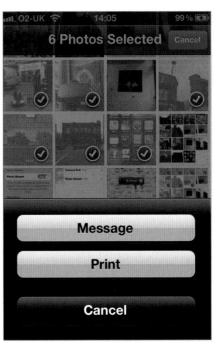

6: Share or print
You could also choose to message or print them from Photo Stream. This simply involves choosing a different button after having selected your images.

Difficulty: Beginner   Time needed: 2 minutes

Learn to tag a photo location on your iPhone

Discover where images were taken using Location Services

There is no easier way to track the advancement of technology in the last 20 years than through cameras. Years ago, taking a photo involved film, chemists and developing, while praying for a good picture. Now you can snap, edit and sort on the device itself within seconds of capturing your images. What's more, managing your photos and labelling them used to involve scrawling details on to the back of the hard copies, but with your iPhone's Camera app you can get instant records of where each photo was taken by ensuring that the Location Services are activated.

Once you have turned on Location Services for the Camera app, any snaps that you take will be marked as pins on Google Maps, which forms part of the Photos app. So you can pinch to zoom in and instantly see which images were taken where. The only downside of these standard apps is that there is no way to add more descriptive text to the images, such as specific locations. However, there are plenty of free apps that allow you to do just that in the App Store. Enter a search for key words such as 'Photo' and 'Tag' and you should find a variety of apps to suit the need to add more detail to your pictures.

Photos | View the location tags of your photographs

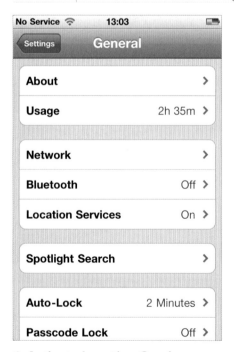

1: Activate Location Services
From your iPhone's Home screen, tap Settings and scroll down the page, then select General. Now tap Location Services, then move the slider to On.

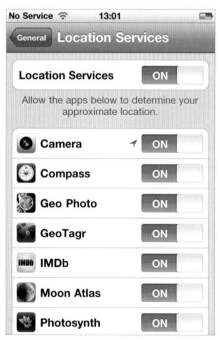

2: Switch on Camera
In Location Services is a list of your iPhone apps that use Location Services. Ensure the slider next to Camera is slid to 'On' and return to your Home screen.

3: Launch camera
Launch the Camera app and take photos. Don't forget to turn the flash on, if required, and then tap the large camera icon or the volume up button to take pictures.

View your tags
Keep track of where your photos were taken

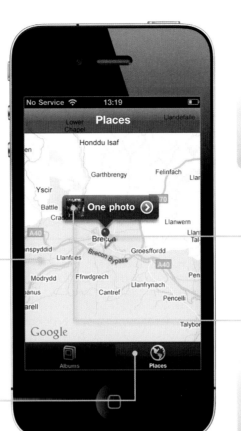

Geotags
The locations of where each of your photos were taken will be marked as pins on Google Maps for easy reference

Maps
You can only view the Google Maps in 'classic' format, but you can zoom in and out by pinching the screen

Get descriptive
Unfortunately, there is currently no way to add descriptive text to your photos using the standard Camera or Photos apps, but thankfully there are plenty of free apps available that do. Photo Name for example, allows you to take photos and caption them in-app before sharing them with your friends.

Switch to album
Options at the bottom of the page allow you to instantly switch between your photo albums and the places where they were taken

Instant access
You can tap on the pins to see which photos were taken at the respective location and switch straight to the album to see them in detail

4: Open Photos
From your Home screen, tap on the Photos app to open up Camera Roll to see thumbnails. Now tap on a thumbnail to see the chosen image in full screen.

5: Go to Places
Tap the Places option found at the bottom of the Camera Roll page for a Google Maps page with pins placed in the locations that all of your photos were captured.

6: View tags
Pinch the screen to zoom in on the pins for map readouts of the locations your images were taken or tap on the pins for a list of the pictures taken there.

Difficulty: Beginner   Time needed: 15 minutes

Edit your videos

Discover how you can make simple edits to video footage captured on your iPhone

As you will have discovered, your iPhone is a fantastic digital camera, enabling you to capture moments at the drop of a hat, but it also functions brilliantly as a video camera, allowing you to record reams of quality footage.

Recording a video on your iPhone is simply a case of opening your Camera app, swiping the slider at the bottom of the screen to the video camera icon, and then pressing record. What you perhaps didn't know is that you can then open your Photos app to not only watch your recorded movies, but edit them too. This quick and easy process is done via the frame slider, which appears at the top of the screen when you are viewing a movie. You can move this

slider along to fast track between frames, but if you tap the right-hand edge you can access an extra option to trim your movies. When you enter 'trim' mode, the edge of the slider will turn yellow and you will be able to pinch frames to select an area to trim, allowing you to cut any flab from your flicks and ensure that the finished products are nicely cropped. Once you are done, you can then share your movies with other people via email, MMS messages or, if you're particularly proud of them, by uploading them straight to YouTube from within the Photos app.

The whole process is a simple task, and we will guide you through it every step of the way in the following tutorial.

Photos | Trimming your videos

1: Open your Camera Roll
Locate your Photos app and then launch it. Once it is running, access your Camera Roll to display all of the photos and videos currently stored on your device.

2: Open a video
Browse through your Camera Roll and tap on a video to open it. Videos will be marked with a small video camera icon and a figure to indicate the running time.

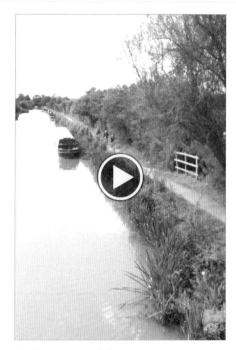

3: Play your video
When a video is open, tap the 'play' icon in the middle of the screen to view it. It is a good idea to view a video in its entirety before making cuts, so you know what you're working with.

Edit on the move

Save space on your device by trimming your videos to their optimum length

Camera Roll
All of your photos and videos are stored in the Camera Roll of your iPhone's Photos app. Tap 'Camera Roll' in the top corner to return to your library

Your video
Tap on a video to view it in full screen in the main window, and then play or pause it via the controls at the bottom of the screen

Share your movies
Once you have edited your videos, you can share them by tapping the icon to the left on the bar at the bottom of the screen. From here, you can email the video to other people or send it in an MMS message, or you can upload it straight to YouTube from within the app.

Clipping
Tap the right-hand edge of the frame slider to start trimming your videos, then pinch or expand on an area to choose the sections you wish to trim

Frame slider
The frame slider at the top of the screen allows you to swipe quickly through every frame of your video to fast track to the points you want

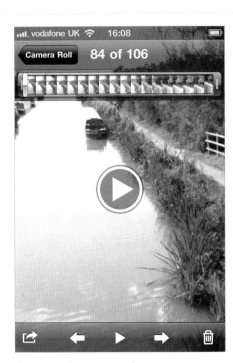

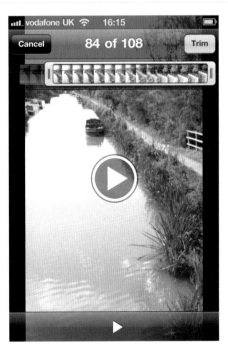

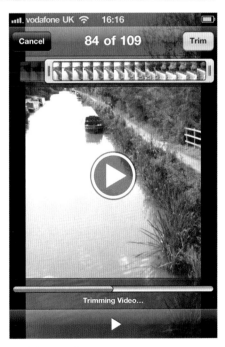

4: Move between frames
Tap the screen to display the full interface, and then you'll notice that there is a scene select slider at the top of the screen. Slide your finger up and down to move between frames.

5: Trim your selection
Tap the right-hand edge of the slider and it will turn yellow and a new 'Trim' option will appear. Now slide the edges together to highlight the portion of the film you would like to save.

6: Trim and save
Once you have made your selection, tap 'Trim' and then choose to trim the original movie or save your edit as a new clip. Make your selection and the changes will be applied.

Difficulty: Intermediate   **Time needed:** 15 minutes

Re-download purchased apps for free

You can easily access all of your previous purchases and download them at any time

As you'll no doubt know, the apps you use on a regular basis go in and out of favour just as favourite music, TV shows and websites do. So you may find yourself deleting the out-of-favour apps in favour of something fresh and new – but that doesn't mean that at some point you won't fancy having a bash at that particular classic game or cool utility again in the future. One of the great new features of the latest version of iOS is the ability to see the apps that you have previously purchased. Furthermore, you can also re-download these at any time. This is actually pretty easy to achieve as you always

download apps using the same account and password, so Apple can easily track what belongs to you. All they had to do to set this system up was to provide a place to do it inside the App Store app that ships with every iPhone. Your purchase history is actually tucked away in the Updates section so it's not immediately obvious, but once you've found it you can scroll through your whole back catalogue of apps and grab any of them at any time and at no extra cost. We recommend that you do this using a Wi-Fi connection, otherwise the huge size of particular apps could result in some serious data charges.

App Store | Get by-gone apps

1: Load it
Load the App Store, make sure that you have the Featured tab at the bottom of the window selected, and then scroll to the very bottom of the list.

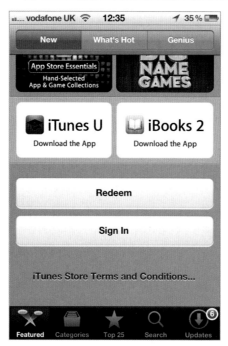

2: Sign in
You will probably be signed in and ready to go by default, but if not, then just enter your registered iTunes email address and password to get started.

3: Reset your password
Select the Use Existing Apple ID option and then enter your password. If you can't remember your password hit the iForgot button to have it reset.

Get downloading
You can easily populate your iPhone directly from the cloud

Go mad
As long as you have enough space, you can download as many apps as you want from your account. Organise them in folders to keep things neat

Watch the Wi-Fi
Make sure you are on Wi-Fi when downloading apps, otherwise it could cost you a fortune in data costs, not to mention take a really long time to download them

Performance
While apps are downloading you may find a drop in performance of your iPhone, which is because the writing of data is taking up precious power from your processor

Watch it happen
You can keep track of your downloads as they happen. Some apps will take no time at all but big apps, like some games, can take quite a while

On your computer
If you want to download a whole batch of apps, it can be quicker to do so on your home computer using iTunes. The process is the same. Login to your account and then find the purchased section so you can download the apps.

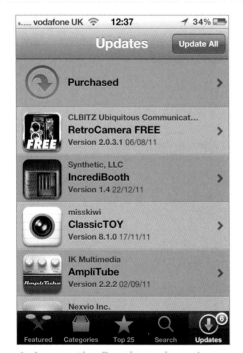

4: Access the Purchased section
Once you have signed in, just tap on the right-hand tab called Updates and, at the top of that screen, you will see a Purchased section. Tap on this section.

5: Get looking
You are now able to see all of the apps that you have ever purchased. Use the tab at the top to see just those that are not currently on your iPhone.

6: Make the decision
Once you have decided which app deserves to be back on your iPhone, tap the cloud button to the right, and your download will begin. It's as simple as that!

Difficulty: Intermediate   Time needed: 10 minutes

Customise your Notification Center

Ensure that you never miss a thing in your work, play or social loop by setting up your own personalised Notification Center

Your iPhone has always been good at notifying you about updates, messages, events and so on. In iOS 4, however, the way in which these messages were conveyed was sometimes quite intrusive, with a message box appearing in the middle of the screen. But iOS 5 really embraces the concept of notifications, and the new and improved system features an enhanced suite to allow you to tailor all aspects of how your device goes about communicating messages to you.

Now, you can get messages, notifications, news and the latest scores delivered to the top of your screen without disturbing what you're doing. All you have to do to set up your own personalised Notification Center is go to Settings, choose the apps, the order they appear, and the manner in which they alert you. To stay in the loop, swipe down from the top of the screen, and you'll be presented with a list of notifications for all of the apps you have featured. Here, we show you how to get the most out of this great new feature.

Notification Center | How to set up and use your Notification Center

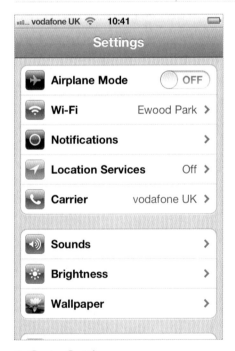

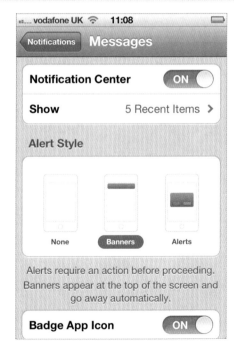

1: Go to Settings
From the Home screen, tap Settings, which is housed in your dock by default, then choose Notifications from the list. You will then be taken through to the main preferences screen.

2: Add items
In Settings, you can choose which apps are featured. To add new apps to your Notification Center, scroll down to the 'Not In…' section, tap an app, then turn Notification Center 'On'.

3: Tailor notification options
Tap the arrow next to an app, and you will see options specific to that app. Choose how many items related to that app are displayed and where the alerts appear on your screen.

Setting up your Notification Center

Tailoring the news feed that is all about you

Badge icons
This slider will determine whether the icon for the app that is notifying you is displayed in the alert. It looks better if they are on

Recent item number
Under 'Show' you can select how many items are shown in that particular app's section in Notification Center, from one to twenty

Switch on
To get alerts for particular apps, ensure the Notification Center slider is switch to 'On' in each app you wish to see featured

Sorting your apps
You can sort your apps on the Notification Center Settings screen by Time or Manually. Sorting by Time means that the order of alerts is based on the time they arrive. You can manually arrange the order of your Notifications by tapping Edit and then rearranging the apps by dragging them.

Alert Style
You can decide how alerts are conveyed to you; either by the standard style Alert, via a non-intrusive Banner, or no notifications at all

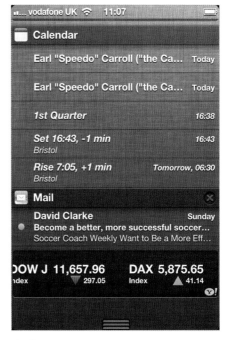

4: Access Notification Center
To access your Notification Center from your Home screen, swipe down from the top of the screen to call up a window of notifications based on the options you've selected.

5: Prepare for alerts
Notifications arrive in the form of a message at the top of the screen, and don't intrude with the app you are currently using. For example, they won't stop any videos currently playing.

6: Go to app
If you need to respond to a notification, or reply to an email, then tap it in your Notification Center, and you will instantly be taken to the specific app to carry out your actions.

The iPhone Book **85**

App used: Facebook Chat+ **Price:** £0.69/$0.99 **Difficulty:** Beginner **Time needed:** 5 minutes

Talk to friends with Facebook Chat+

Stay in touch with friends more easily than ever before

Facebook works fantastically well in app form, allowing you to update your status, follow your friends and chat, but if you operate on a tight schedule and want to streamline your chats to be even easier, Facebook Chat+ (Alexander Buharsky, £0.69/$0.99) is a great app for fast talkers.

By connecting Facebook Chat+ with your regular Facebook account, you can instantly see which of your friends are online and start chatting immediately. Simply write what you want into the text field and you can fire off messages within seconds of launching the app. So far, so standard, as the Facebook app

enables you to do that. However, Facebook Chat+ differs by allowing you to add more personality to your messages in the form of a range of emoticons, and it features voice recognition capabilities. By tapping on the microphone icon in the text input field, you can command the app to record your messages and, within seconds, it will convert your spoken words into text and add them to the text field for you to send off. It's fabulously intuitive and will make staying in touch easier than ever before. In this tutorial, we guide you through the process of setting up the app and sending your first messages.

Facebook Chat+ | Chat with your Facebook friends

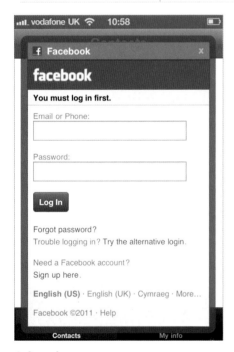

1: Log in
When you launch the app for the first time, you will be required to enter your Facebook details. Do so and then grant Facebook Chat+ permission to access your account.

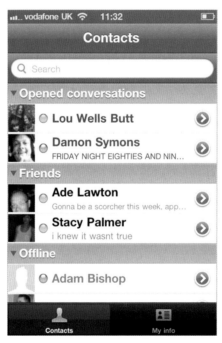

2: Browse your contacts
After logging in, you will be presented with a full list of contacts from your Facebook account, divided into who's online and who isn't. Tap on someone who is online to start a conversation.

3: Type a message
Type what you want to say into the text window and then press 'Send' to fire off your message. Your messages and the replies will be displayed in the main window.

Chatting freely on Facebook Chat+

Why this app is a quick and easy way to stay in touch with your Facebook buddies

Add some expression
You can attach and embed emoticons to your messages by tapping on the smiley face icon and then choosing from an extensive list

Stay logged in
By default the app will log out of your Facebook account every time you quit, so if you intend to use Facebook Chat+ often you can stay permanently logged in by adjusting the slider on the 'My Info' page.

Text window
If you tap the text field, you'll bring up your iPhone keyboard to quickly type out messages to your friends

Your conversations
The messages you send and the ones you receive back will be displayed in the main message window

Voice recognition
Why type your messages when you can say them? Tap the microphone icon and record a message that the app will then convert into text for you

---

4: Add emoticons
If you wish to punctuate your messages with emoticons, tap the smiley face icon next to the text field and choose an icon from the list. This will then be embedded in your message.

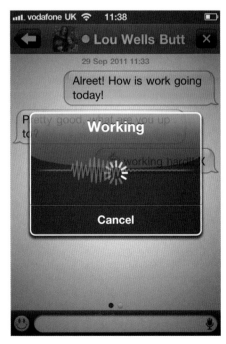

5: Use your voice
If you don't have time to type messages, tap the microphone icon in the text field and then speak what you want to say. When you stop, the app will convert your message into text.

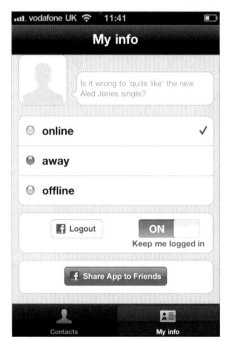

6: Update your status
You can also update your Facebook status from within this app. Tap on the 'My Info' icon in the bottom-right corner and tap on the speech bubble to add text.

App used: Twitter Price: Free Difficulty: Beginner Time needed: 5 minutes

Master Twitter integration on your phone

Now that Twitter is integrated into iOS 5, we show you how to share your thoughts and links from within your favourite apps

There's little doubt that Twitter is a social phenomenon. This simple application allows you to share thoughts – or 'tweets' – with people around the world almost as soon as they enter your head, and likewise, see what's on the minds of people that you choose to follow.

The advent of smartphones has taken this concept to the next level by allowing you to tweet at any time, wherever you are in the world, making it easier than ever to speak your mind. Now, the tweeting process just got

even easier with iOS 5. Twitter is integrated seamlessly into Apple's new operating system; simply sign in, then begin tweeting directly from your favourite apps. You no longer need to open a specific Twitter app, find a photo to upload or copy links from your web browser; simply do it directly from within the app. It's so easy that your Twitter activity will increase dramatically once you get to grips with it. In this tutorial, we guide you through setting up Twitter integration, and how to tweet from your favourite apps.

Twitter | Tweet from within your favourite apps

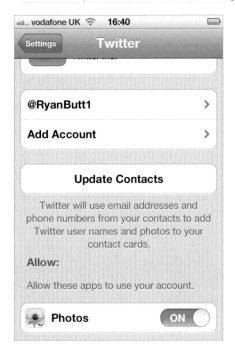

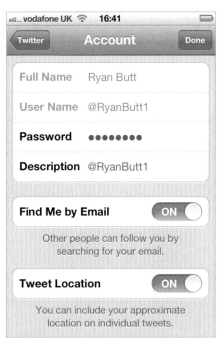

1: Go to Settings

Choose Settings, then tap on the Twitter option to bring up the app's preferences. If you don't already have Twitter installed, tap Install and add an account.

2: Log in

Now enter your details – including your username and password – adjust the 'Find Me by Email' and Tweet Location options, and then tap Done.

3: Tweet in Safari

Open up Safari. To tweet about a page, tap the Add Bookmark option, and then choose Tweet. A link to the Safari page will be added to your tweet.

Integrating Twitter

Tweet easily from other apps

● Install the app
When setting up Twitter integration, you must first ensure that the app is installed. You can do this from within the Twitter section in Settings

● Update contacts
Twitter can cleverly use email addresses and phone numbers from your contacts to add Twitter usernames and photos to your contact cards. Just hit 'Update Contacts'

● Your details
Once you have entered your username and password, you will stay logged in to Twitter across all of the apps that integrate with it

Camera comments
If your iPhone 4 or iPad 2 device has iOS 5 installed, then you can also tweet from within the Camera app, allowing you to upload, comment and caption your pictures almost as soon as they are captured. Keeping others informed of your actions has never been so easy.

● Grant permissions
In order to allow Twitter to become integrated with other apps, you must grant permission for particular apps to use your Twitter account

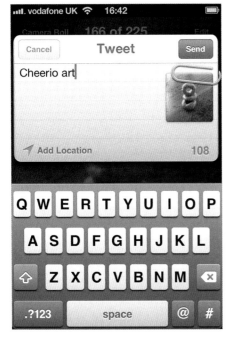

4: Tweet in Photos
When viewing an image in the Photos app, tap the share icon and then select Tweet. Any pictures that you tweet about will be added as a link.

5: Tweet in YouTube
You can also share videos in YouTube by tapping the Share button at the top of the viewing window, then Tweet. A link will be added to your message.

6: Tweet in Maps
If you want to tweet your location or places of interest, start by tapping on your current location in Maps, then the 'i' icon. Choose Share Location, then Tweet.

App used: TripAdvisor   Price: Free   Difficulty: Beginner   Time needed: 20 minutes

Plan a trip using your iPhone

Looking to get away from it all? With TripAdvisor, you can make sure you find the best getaways at the keenest prices

As little as 20 years ago, most of us probably planned our holidays with the help of a high street travel agent. But access to cheap flights and the ability to book holidays directly has enabled us to take control of our travel arrangements. The TripAdvisor website (**www.tripadvisor.com**) has earned itself a good reputation as a reliable service for travellers, particularly as it features unbiased reviews submitted by fellow travellers. Now add to this mix the iPhone, which has made a name for itself as a useful travel companion in its own right.

The iPhone's TripAdvisor app squeezes the website into your pocket by offering a gateway to the same resources as the web version, in a neater format. You can search for local hotels, restaurants and other attractions, and it will even find flights for you. It also offers access to online forums for user advice.

Additionally, the iPhone adds extra power because it's truly mobile and offers location awareness. In practice, it means you can take the iPhone on a trip and it can interrogate TripAdvisor to find nearby hotels or restaurants. Chances are you'll find it indispensable.

TripAdvisor | Plan a perfect break

1: Choose a location
Tap the Hotels link and enter the city or address to which you're travelling. TripAdvisor offers a list of suggestions for you. Tap one and then tap Find Hotels.

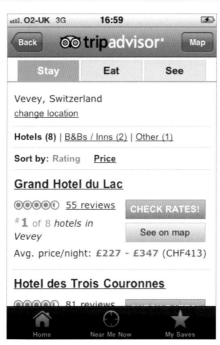

2: Find the best and cheapest
TripAdvisor searches its database and divides results into hotels and guest houses, ordered by price or rating. The results include a link to book a room.

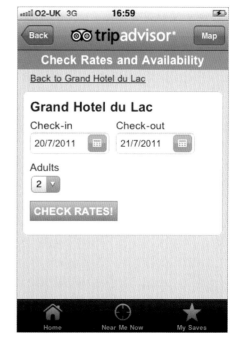

3: Book the hotel
Tap on the 'See on map' button to see where the hotel is, and 'Check Rates!' to see the price and availability. You can even book the hotel from here.

TripAdvisor travel tips
Getting the most out of the app

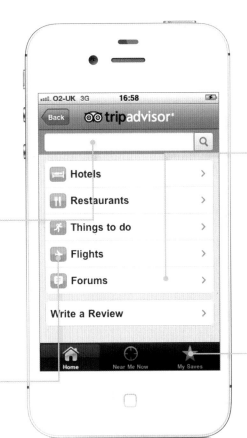

General information
Want general information about a destination? Enter its name here and tap the Search icon and TripAdvisor will mine its database for everything about it

Flight control
You can even search for cheap holiday flights. Tap here and enter your travel details and TripAdvisor will search its travel partners for available flights

Travellers' tales
For general research about your trip, visit the TripAdvisor forums. This area offers non-specific advice, tips and chat organised by region or topic

What's the catch?
TripAdvisor is a great free resource – so how does it make money? In two ways: from on-site adverts, as well as through affiliate agencies, such as airlines and hotel booking services, which supply the results whenever you search TripAdvisor.

My Saves
It's easy to pick up great travel titbits. If you click the Save button on any pages, the results are stored and can be opened here

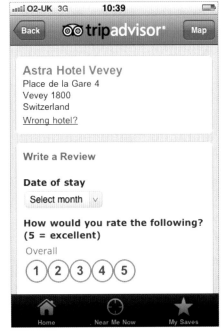

4: Find local restaurants
You'll be hungry after your journey. On the Home screen, tap Restaurants. Check 'Find restaurants near me now', and filter by cuisine and price.

5: Look at things to do
To find local interests, tap 'Things to do', check 'Find attractions near me now' and pick a type of attraction. The results are organised by rating or distance.

6: Speak your mind
Tap 'Write a Review' and enter the name of the hotel, restaurant or activity. Rate it based on given criteria and add your own comments to help others.

Demo: Reverse Words

App used: Word Lens   **Price:** Free (with in-app purchases)   **Difficulty:** Beginner   **Time needed:** 5 minutes

Translate text and understand foreign signs

Translating foreign languages has just become easier than ever before with the Word Lens app for iPhone

Learning a new language is never easy and can take months or years of studying. Phrase books have long been a staple accessory of people travelling abroad, but now there is a new way. Word Lens is an ingenious app that can translate foreign language words by simply holding up an iPhone camera to the text. It replaces the words you are viewing on the screen with a literal translation and the characters are readable so you can see what the translation is at a glance.

This technology can be used in many circumstances such as reading road signs abroad, understanding menus and anywhere that requires translation. In theory you could even read a foreign language book using Word Lens, but at the time of writing only translations between English and Spanish are available. You need to buy Spanish to English and English to Spanish separately as in-app purchases, with each costing you £6.99/$9.99. Hopefully further languages will be available in the future which will increase the flexibility. The potential is great and the implementation clever, though, making sifting through various phrase books a thing of the past.

Words Lens | Translate with your camera

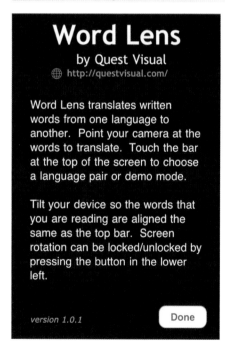

1: Get started

When you first download and open the app you should tap the 'i' at the bottom of the screen which offers a guide. The app is exceptionally easy to use.

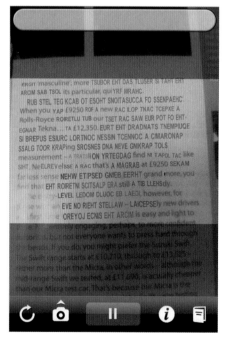

2: Translate

Hold up your camera to a piece of foreign text. It can be a road sign, magazine or anything typed, however, handwritten text is difficult to translate visually.

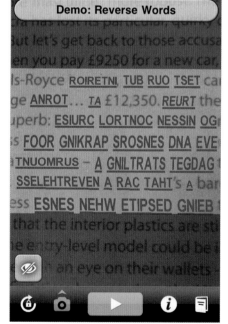

3: See the results

Translated words are highlighted in blue when you press pause, showing words that the app doesn't recognise. The success rate is high, though, so you can get the gist.

Use the main translation interface

A look at the functions in Word Lens

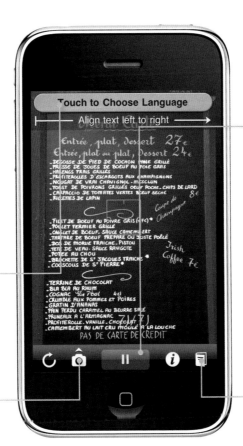

Languages
Hopefully in the future you will be able to select from multiple languages that should cover every foreign trip

Camera
Because the camera is used to view text, you can still adjust the flash settings and zoom in as needed

Pausing
When you tap the pause button, the translated words are highlighted in blue. You can check omissions easily, but the general meaning will come forth

Not too literal
No translation tool will be 100 per cent accurate due to grammatical differences, but an app like this will suffice on most occasions. If you decide that you do want literal translations, you will need to do some learning and lots of it.

Manual translation
You can manually translate words by typing them into the app. This is a simple function that is similar to other apps, but it works very well

4: Tweak it
You can tweak the app by tapping the camera button at the bottom. This lets you select portions of the screen with autofocus, use the flash or zoom.

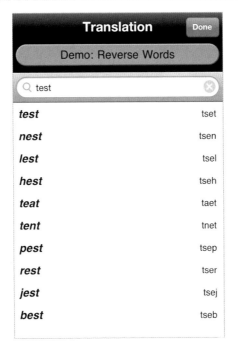

5: Manually translate
You can manually type in words to get their true meaning by tapping the icon at the bottom. This is a feature that comes in handy time and time again.

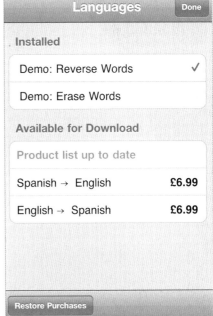

6: Make it work
Tapping the bar at the top gives you the option to purchase two-way translations and restore your purchases if you have had to reset your device for whatever reason.

Productivity

Get organised and manage your tasks with the iPhone

98 Back up your important phone data with iCloud

102 iOS 5 makes surfing Safari much easier

106 Quickly send emails with Siri's voice control

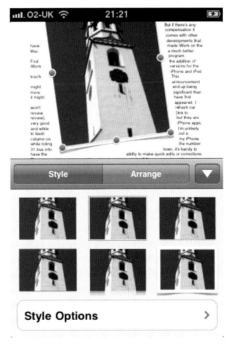

114 Add images to your Pages documents

"The iPhone can speed up processes and tasks"

Sync your apps with iCloud

Your iCloud can work wonders behind the scenes to wirelessly move your documents between devices

Once you have set up your free iCloud account, take a look at how this service works in tandem with your iPhone apps.

There is no disputing that iCloud is a very useful service that can benefit you in myriad ways and make life significantly easier, but unless you know exactly how then there seems little point in activating your free account. For example, should you activate Photo Stream if you don't take any photos? And is it worth

switching the Documents & Files feature on if you don't have any iWork apps on your Mac? In this tutorial we will guide you through each of the app options that you are presented with on the iCloud Settings screen and also describe what each feature does. From this you can decide if you need it on or not and then go about utilising the ones that you do activate. But, however you decide to use iCloud, before too long you will wonder how you ever managed without it.

> "There is no disputing that iCloud is a very useful service that can benefit you in myriad ways and make life significantly easier"

iCloud | Which apps should you activate?

1: Mail, Contacts & Calendars
If you lead a busy lifestyle and use multiple iOS 5 devices then you should enable all three of these options so that calendar events, contacts and emails are synced and updated.

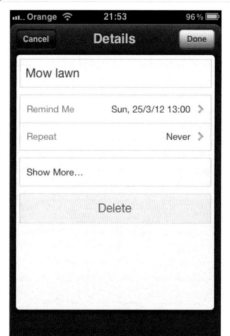

2: Reminders
Reminders is a new free app that lets you make 'to do' lists and set reminders. By activating it in iCloud then all of your devices will remind you, not just the one you set the reminder on.

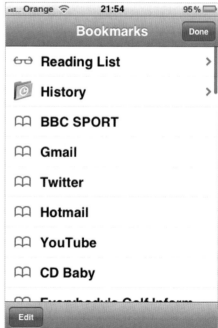

3: Safari Bookmarks
Enabling Bookmarks ensures all items stored in your Safari Reading List are synced across devices, making it easy to browse on your iPhone and continue on an iPad, for example.

Activate iCloud apps

Syncing apps to iCloud is as easy as moving sliders with your fingers

● Your account
You can view your iCloud account information by tapping on the Account section at the top of the iCloud Settings screen

● Extra options?
The Photo Stream and Documents & Data options have extra screens. There are no additional options associated with them, just more detailed explanations

● Enabling apps
To utilise the iCloud features of your apps, to sync info and data across devices, simply move the slider of each app to the 'On' position

● Storage used
You can see how much of your free five-gigabyte allocation is being used by clicking on the 'Storage & Backup' option

Peace of mind
If you mislay your iPhone, then worry not. As long as you enable the 'Find My iPhone' option on the iCloud Settings screen, the position of your device will be stored in your iCloud and can be accessed from any computer web browser by going to **www.icloud.com.**

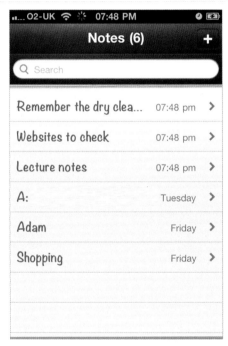

4: Notes
Moving the 'Notes' slider to 'On' will ensure any notes that you make through the Notes app on one device will be synced and made available to read and edit on other devices.

5: Photo Stream
A brilliant feature that does away with the need to email images between devices. If you take a photo on your iPhone, with Photo Stream it will appear in Photos on other devices in seconds.

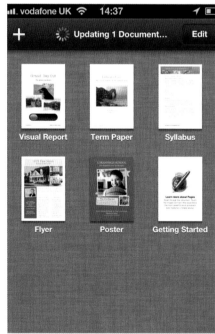

6: Documents & Data
If you have the same iWork apps on your Mac or iPhone, this ensures any changes you make on your iPhone will be reflected on other devices, without needing to save or transfer.

Difficulty: Beginner **Time needed:** 5 minutes

Use iCloud to back up your iPhone

With iCloud, you can back up all of your important iPhone data to your own virtual hard drive

 Your iPhone is like a bank vault where all kinds of stuff is stored. So what happens if your iPhone gets lost or goes awry? Nothing, that's what. Thanks to iCloud, all of your data is automatically backed up and kept safely in your own cloud storage space. When your iPhone is connected to a power source and a Wi-Fi network, all of your media, photos, videos, settings, app data and messages are backed up.

When you set up a new iOS device or need to restore the information on the one you already have, iCloud Backup does all the heavy lifting. All you have to do is ensure that your device is connected to Wi-Fi, enter your Apple ID and all of your important data will appear on your device without you having to worry about a single thing.

As you will have read elsewhere in this bookazine, the benefits of using iCloud are vast, and the way in which it goes about its business in the background without you having to worry is just another prime example of how Apple is striving to make your life easier.

iCloud | Activate iCloud and back up your data

1: Update to iOS 5
iCloud is a service that comes as part of iOS 5, so connect your device to your computer through iTunes and check to ensure you have the latest free software update on your device.

2: Launch Settings
From your iPhone's Home screen, launch your Settings app, and navigate to the category called 'iCloud'. Tap on this and then enter your Apple ID and password.

3: Set up
Once your personal iCloud has been set up and you have selected which apps you would like to sync, tap on the 'Storage & Backup' option at the bottom of the list.

Backing up with iCloud

Once activated, your iCloud will back up your stuff automatically

Instant backup
You can back up your data by tapping the 'Backup Now' option. Do this if you change your settings or buy new media

Progress bar
When your device is backing up, a progress bar will appear that shows how far along the process it is. You can cancel the backup at any time

Manage your space
You can see how your free 5GB allocation of cloud storage space is used by tapping on the 'Manage Storage' option

Manage your storage
By tapping on the 'Storage & Backup' option in the iCloud Settings screen and then going to 'Manage Storage', you'll be able to see exactly how your iCloud is used with individual breakdowns of how much of your free 5GB of space your apps use. If you find that you need to purchase more space then you can do so through this screen.

Backup
When the 'iCloud Backup' option is turned on, all settings, documents, media and photos will be automatically backed up when your device is connected to a power supply and Wi-Fi

4: Turn on Backup
On this screen you will be able to monitor and manage your iCloud storage space, but more importantly you will see an option called 'iCloud Backup'. Ensure that the slider is moved to 'On'.

5: Wait for the activation
You'll be presented with a message saying your iPhone will no longer sync to iTunes when connected to your computer. Tap 'OK' and wait while the Backup feature is activated.

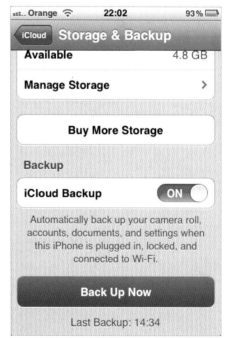

6: Start backing up
Your iPhone will now back up when connected to a power source and a Wi-Fi network, but you can perform the backup whenever you want by accessing this screen and tapping 'Backup Now'.

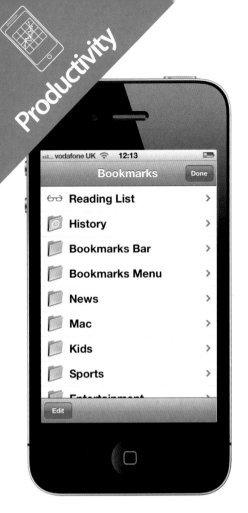

Difficulty: Beginner Time needed: 5 minutes

Get the most from bookmarks

The iPhone has many uses, but one of its main strengths is browsing the web. Here's how to get the most out of it

 The iPhone is great for many things, and the extra applications available for it expand its usability even further. Some of the built-in applications will get more use than anything you download from the App Store, however. One of the apps you are likely to use more often than any other is Safari.

Though there are less features on the iPhone version of Safari compared to the desktop, there's still a lot you can do with the application. Holding the internet in your hands is great, and really changes the way you browse and interact with the web. Though Safari shares its name with the Mac and PC equivalents, it's not exactly the same as those applications. The iPhone version of Safari has been tweaked to work much better with the touch interface. With your free iCloud account, you can also sync your bookmarks with the iPhone and Safari on your computer, as well as add sites to your home screen for easier access. Here, we'll show you how to maximise Safari's bookmarking potential.

Safari | Get to grips with bookmarks in Safari on the iPhone

1: Add a website
Navigate to a website on your home screen. When it has loaded, tap on the middle icon on the bottom bar and tap Add to Home Screen.

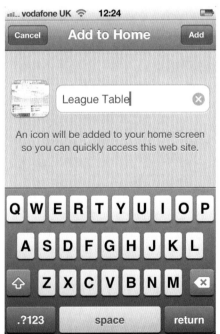

2: Give your icon a name
When you tap on Add to Home Screen, it will add the title of the page, but you can edit this if you wish. Tap Add when you're done.

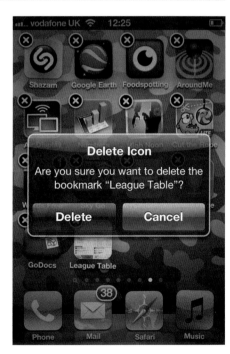

3: Get rid of a home screen icon
If you're not using your bookmarked home screen icon very much, it's easy to get rid of it. Tap and hold until the 'X' appears, and tap it.

4: Add a bookmark
You may be familiar with internet bookmarks, and can add them on the iPhone,. Tap the same button on the toolbar, then Add Bookmark.

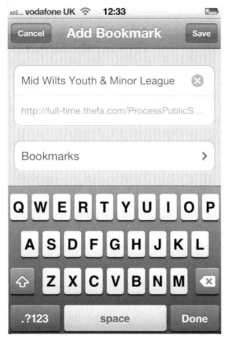

5: Name your bookmark
You will have to give your new bookmark a name. This will be automatically chosen, but you can easily change it.

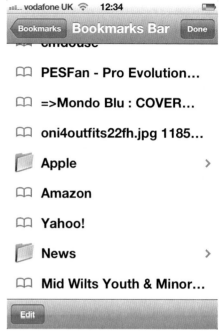

6: Get to your bookmarks
To view bookmarks, tap the icon to the right of the middle button. They'll be under the History and Bookmarks Menu and Bar folders.

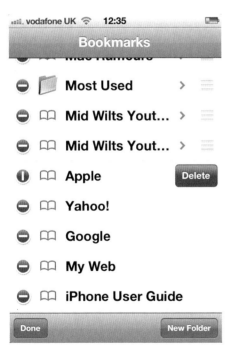

7: Delete a bookmark
To remove a bookmark, tap on the Bookmarks icon, and then Edit. A red icon with a '–' symbol will appear; tap it, and then the Delete option.

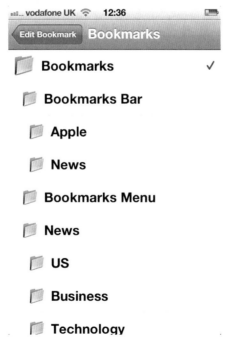

8: Move the bookmark
To move a bookmark, tap Edit and then tap on your bookmark. Choose a folder in the field below the address.

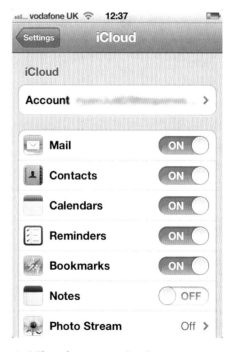

9: iCloud not syncing?
If you've got an iCloud account and find it's not syncing, go to the Settings menu, tap on iCloud and ensure that Bookmarks are toggled on.

Difficulty: Beginner Time needed: 5 minutes

Get to know the new features in Safari

Discover how the already fantastic experience of surfing the web on your device is made even easier with iOS 5

 Surfing the web on your Apple device has always been a simple and pleasurable experience, but iOS 5 adds some welcome tweaks to ensure that the experience is even easier. Two of the most prominent enhancements are Reader and Reading List.

With Reading List, you can save articles to read offline, and upload them to your iCloud so that they get pushed to all of your other iOS 5 devices. This means that you can start reading an article on your iPhone during your commute home, and then pick it up exactly where you left off on your iPad when you arrive. Reader supplies a similarly handy service by allowing you to read stripped-down versions of articles. If you want to focus on a particular story without being distracted by clutter such as adverts, then you can tap the 'Reader' icon in the address bar, and get a new, cleaner take on the article, as everything apart from the text and related images are wiped away. Take time to familiarise yourself with these new features, and take your surfing to a whole new level.

Safari | Utilising the many features of Safari

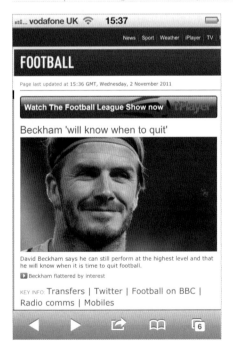

1: Launch Safari
When you launch Safari, you can tap on the address field to go to a new site, and then use pinch gestures on the screen to zoom in on the content and get a better view.

2: Open a new page
You can open a new page without closing the current one; just tap the Pages button in the bottom right corner, and then tap 'New Page'. Flick between pages from this screen.

3: Use your Reader
You can read certain stories without the page clutter, like adverts. If a page works, then a 'Reader' icon will appear in the address bar. Tap this icon to go to your simplified page.

Find your way around Safari

Little enhancements that make a big difference

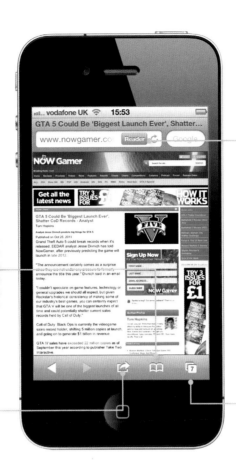

● Reading List
A great new Safari enhancement is Reading List. If you're running short on time, add an article to your list, and you'll be able to finish it later – even on a different device

● Tweet from within
With Twitter integrated in iOS 5, you can tweet from within your favourite apps without having to copy links into a separate Twitter app

● Safari Reader
To read certain articles without clutter, such as pictures or ads, tap the Reader icon in the address bar, and all non-article material will be stripped away

Cloud connect
Safari works with your own personal iCloud, meaning that any articles you add to your Reading List are synced to your iCloud and stored. You can start reading them on an iPhone, and pick them up where you left off on your iPad later.

● Your pages
All of the webpages that you currently have open will be accessible from this icon. Tap on it and scroll to the currently open page you want to visit

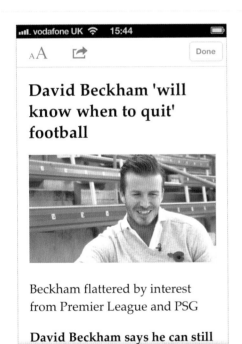

4: View pages through Reader
Pages viewed through Reader will contain only text and images, making it easier to read without running the risk of tapping on an ad. When you have finished reading, tap 'Done'.

5: Save to your Reading List
You can save pages that you are reading to your Reading List to finish later. Tap the Bookmarks icon, and then choose 'Add to Reading List'. Your stories will then be saved like bookmarks.

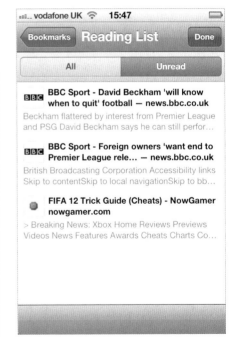

6: Access your Reading List
When you want to return to a story, tap the Bookmarks icon, then choose 'Reading List'. All stories will be pushed to your other iOS 5 devices via iCloud when activated.

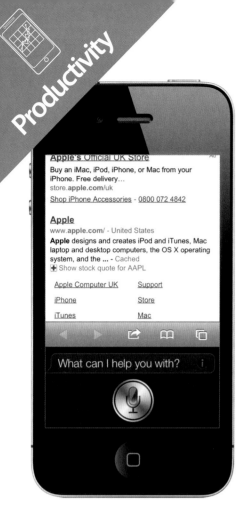

Difficulty: Beginner   Time needed: 2 minutes

Search with Siri

Aside from dictating text, Siri is also linked to the web, meaning you can search and more using voice control

 Although Siri's basic functions are quite simple to understand, you can only get a proper feeling for what it is capable of by playing around with it and trying out new phrases to unearth the possibilities of the technology. Most commands can be traced back to one or more trigger phrases that get things rolling.

For searching, however, you need to be more specific. While saying the word 'search' alone to prompt Siri will not work, you can always follow up with your chosen search by saying something like, 'Search for iPhone 4S'.

After a few seconds of working, Siri will dictate your search term back to you, then ask if you want to search the web. You can either press the search button – which will then open up Safari and perform a Google search – or you can use voice commands to confirm the search.

You can even be more specific by saying something like, 'Search for the best contract details for iPhone 4S', and it will run a Google search for articles and online shops that have decent iPhone 4S deals. It is also possible to search for nearby shops or events in your vicinity using a combination of Siri and Google Maps, although at the time of writing this is only available to iPhone 4S users in America. This feature is, however, due to be rolled out across Europe and elsewhere in the future.

Siri | Running different Siri searches

1: Activate Siri
Activating Siri is as simple as holding down your Home button, or by holding the device to your ear and speaking the command. Siri flashes purple when it is ready to receive phrases.

2: Do simple searches
You can start small by asking Siri to search for a simple phrase, and this prompts Safari to run the search. Simply speak your phrase and tap the search button, or say 'Search the web'.

3: Be more specific
Rather than searching for a simple phrase, you can be more specific. Instead of saying, 'Search iPhone 4S', Siri will still understand if you say, 'Search for cheapest iPhone deals', for example.

Searching in Safari
Your options after performing a Siri web search

Location-based searches
As we've touched upon, Google Maps searches only work using Siri if you're based in America at the time of writing. It's a great function, however, and you can say things like, 'Search for Italian restaurants nearby', and Siri will search for them on Google Maps, and show you where they are.

Google bar
You can type a new search into this bar, or dictate the search term using Siri by tapping the microphone icon on the keypad

New tab
Hitting the new page button will let you open new tabs, and have multiple websites open at the same time, which is great for multitasking

Options button
Tap this icon to print, tweet via your Twitter app, bookmark the link, email the link or add it to your Home screen

Bookmarks button
This icon will let you bookmark the page for future reference, and in this menu you can organise links into specific folders and topics

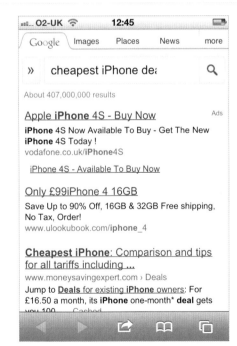

4: Post-search commands
After executing your Siri search, you can bookmark the results in Safari, forward the link to an email address, tweet the results to your Twitter followers, and more.

5: Search for sites
If you know the URL of a site you want to visit in Safari, you can actually dictate the site's address without the 'www' part, and Siri will perform a Google search for the URL.

6: Search for contacts
If you have an address book full of contacts, you can simply start Siri and say, 'Search contacts', followed by the name of the person. Siri will come back with all relevant contact info.

Difficulty: Beginner   Time needed: 5 minutes

Create emails using Siri

Learn how to create, tailor and send detailed email messages at speed using a combination of Siri and classic touch features

 While Siri-enabled iPhone 4S owners can carry out tasks on their device using voice control alone, creating and sending emails to contacts actually requires a little bit of preparation. If you want to create emails and send them to contacts by name using Siri, you will first need to enter their email address into your contacts. Without this, you will be unable to create emails and send them using voice alone.

Once you have added the email address of your chosen contact, you will first need to activate Siri by either holding down your iPhone's Home button or by simply speaking your voice commands into the microphone.

To get the ball rolling, all you have to do is say, 'Create email', and Siri will then ask who you want to send the message to. Say the person's name and, if you have their email address saved in your contacts, Siri will pull the information out and add it to the recipient field.

You will then be prompted to dictate the message's subject field and then the body text. If Siri has misinterpreted your speech at any point, you can tap the message to bring up the email client, and from there you can make amendments using the keypad, or dictate again by tapping the microphone icon on the keyboard. When you are ready, send the email by saying 'Confirm' or by hitting 'Send'.

Siri | Use Siri to create emails

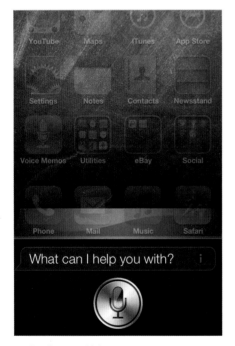

1: Activate Siri
To get started with creating your email, hold down the iPhone Home button until the Siri icon appears on screen. When Siri is ready to accept your commands, it will flash purple.

2: Get started
By saying 'Create email', Siri will start the email creation process. First, it will ask you who you would like to send the email to. You can see your progress in the preview pane at all times.

3: State the recipient
Say the name of the person you want to send the message to. Please note that this will only work if you have their email address saved under their name in your contacts.

Edit your message
Fix typos, elaborate and more

Recipient field
It's important to bear in mind that Siri can only add email contacts by name if you have saved them in your Address Book first

Attaching images
At this time, you are unable to include attachments to emails using Siri. If you need to attach an image, your best bet is to enter your iPhone's photo library, hit the sharing icon to bring up a blank email with the image attached, then hit the microphone icon to dictate the body text in Siri.

Cancel button
Once you enter the iPhone email client, you can't go back to the Siri preview pane. If you need to restart the process, simply hit 'Cancel'

Siri icon
Tap the Siri icon to dictate the message body text, recipients and the subject line. When satisfied, simply hit 'Done' and Siri will type out what you said

Keypad
You can fine tune your message or fix mistakes that Siri has made by using the keypad. This ensures that your messages are typo-free and accurate before sending

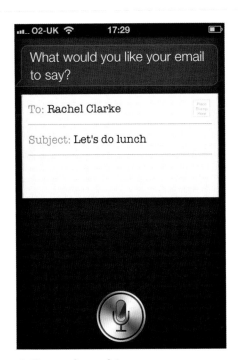

4: Enter the subject
Siri will ask you for the subject line. If Siri fails to understand you, edit this manually by tapping the preview pane. Siri will then ask for your email body text.

5: Dictate body text
Dictate your email body text, and Siri will write what it thinks you said into the preview pane. You can then send by saying 'Send', cancel by saying 'Cancel', or edit by tapping the preview.

6: Some fine tuning
If you need to edit the message, simply tap the preview pane to open the message in your email client. Here you can type amendments, or hit the microphone icon to re-dictate with Siri.

Difficulty: Beginner Time needed: 2 minutes

Create Reminders in Siri

Master the art of Reminders on the iPhone 4S with Siri, and create massive to-do lists in a snap through voice control

 One the newest features of the iPhone 4S, Siri is an innovative and powerful piece of voice recognition software that enables you to perform a multitude of tasks using voice alone. Once you get your iPhone 4S, or update your device to iOS 5, you will notice that there is a new 'Reminders' app icon on your top menu.

This is another new feature that lets you create to-do lists – both intricate or basic – for any task at hand. You can set up reminders using touch, or if you want to do it faster and without navigating multiple menus, you can simply dictate your task to Siri, and it will schedule items automatically.

The usual process of setting up reminders is to hold down the home button until Siri prompts you to speak. You can say something like "Create reminder", and Siri will ask you for further information, such as location, time and the nature of the task.

You can even set up alarms that tell Siri when you want to be reminded. This can be scheduled for a precise time of your choosing – say, the day before the deadline – so you will never forget a chore or errand again. Asking Siri "Do I have any reminders tomorrow" (or on any day) also prompts Siri to tell you what tasks you have on that particular day. It's a smart, efficient and fluid process that works a treat.

Siri | Creating and tailoring reminders

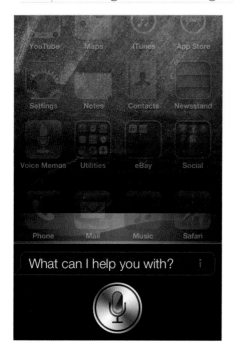

1: Activate Siri
To create a reminder, simply hold down your iPhone's home button or start speaking. If you choose the former method, Siri will flash purple when it is ready to accept your speech input.

2: Prompt the process
Once prompted, if you say "Create Reminder" Siri will flash purple again, and will then ask you what it is you would like to be reminded about. Siri will then dictate it back to you.

3: Describe your reminder
Once you have stated the nature of the reminder to Siri, it will display what you just said in text, and will then ask you when you would like to be reminded.

Expanding your reminder

How to elaborate on your schedule tasks

Remind Me
The reminder time can always be altered after you make an entry. Simply tap this pane to pick a new alarm and edit the entry

Repeat
For frequent events or tasks, you can set repeated reminders that repeat on dates and times of your choosing. Tap this pane to repeat

Priority
Tap this pane to set the importance of the entry from high to low. Higher priority reminders will appear higher on your list

Notes
If you need more information, you can type additional directions or instructions in the notes pane, or you can dictate them using Siri

Adding contacts to reminders
You can create a contact for yourself in your phone's address book, complete with information on your spouse, family, colleagues and more. Once done, go to your iPhone's settings. Select 'General', then Siri. You will see a pane called 'My Info'. Select the contact you created for yourself, and Siri will recognise these people by name, and add their info to your reminders automatically.

4: Confirm the reminder
Once you have dictated all of the relevant information, Siri will display a snapshot of your Reminders page, complete with descriptions, time and date. Say "Confirm" to save.

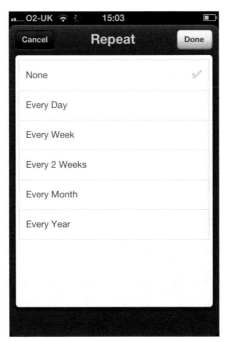

5: Set reminder frequency
Once your reminder is saved, you can repeat the reminder alarm if it is a regular event. Simply go into the Reminders app, locate the entry and select 'Repeat' to re-schedule.

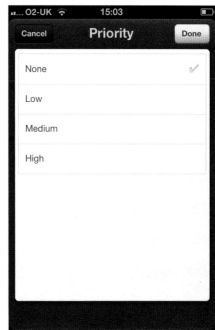

6: Set reminder priority
If you have some tasks that are more important than others, you can actually tailor entries to give them a higher or lower priority, thus pushing them further up or down your task list.

Difficulty: Beginner Time needed: 2 minutes

Book an appointment using Siri on iPhone 4S

Stay organised using Siri's voice functionality, and do it all at speed without tapping the screen once

 Siri is Apple's new voice-activated technology that takes your hands – and tapping keys – out of the equation. It's more than just a hands-free software, however. Siri is fully integrated throughout your device's Contacts, Notes, Messages, Safari browser and more. It's only once you start using Siri that you can appreciate how much easier it makes your life.

One such function is the ability to create and schedule appointments via voice control. Starting Siri is simple in that you either hold down the iPhone's main button, tap the microphone icon on the keyboard, or simply start talking to your device.

There are many stock phrases that trigger an appointment booking, but 'Schedule appointment' is by far the most common. Once you say this, Siri will ask for further information, such as the day, time, and who the meeting is with. Once scheduled, you can elaborate on your appointment by dictating notes such as directions, addresses, or reminders.

The neat thing about Siri is that it will always dictate back to you, meaning that you can edit anything it has failed to pick up correctly. But with a high success rate, this isn't something you will need to worry about often.

Siri | Create an appointment using voice control

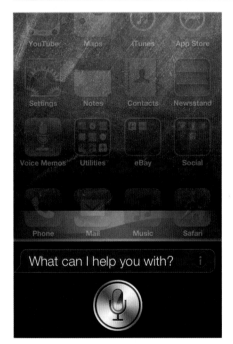

1: Start Siri

Hold down the iPhone's main button or start speaking to start the creation process. Siri will flash purple when it is working out what to say next.

2: Dictate the appointment

Creating the appointment is as simple as saying something like 'Schedule appointment with (person's name) on (date) at (time)'. Siri will process this, and relay what it thinks you said.

3: Confirm the booking

Siri will then ask you to confirm the booking by showing you a preview of your calendar, and asking you to say either 'Cancel' or 'Confirm' to save or discard the appointment.

Tailoring your appointments

Add extra data to make appointments more specific

Manage separate calendars
Hit the Calendar tab to separate work and personal appointments into two distinct schedules. This is handy when looking to keep different bookings separate

Your personal secretary
If you find that you have a hectic schedule, you can ask Siri if you have time free on a particular day by doing just that. Saying something as simple as "Do I have any appointments scheduled tomorrow?" will prompt Siri to list all of your booked appointments on that day. Siri will also warn you of any clashing appointments.

Repeating events
If your meetings are regular, you can re-schedule them easily on repeated, or on very specific days only, by using this tab

Inviting your contacts
Tap the Invitees tab to bring up a text entry pane. Here, you can manually type or dictate names, or select contacts from your address book

Set up alerts
Touch the Alert tab to set a custom alarm to remind you of the event. You can choose from a wide range of timed options

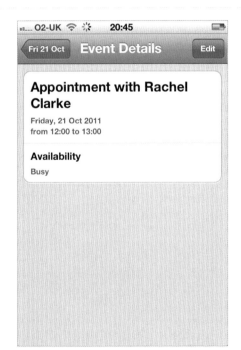

4: Expand the booking
Elaborate further by tapping the calendar preview then pressing the 'Edit' button. This will open up more options to you, ensuring you have all the details you need.

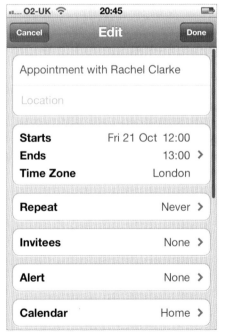

5: Be more descriptive
From this screen, you can input further details such as location, relevant contact details, related URLs and more. You will need to use touch for this section, but you can still dictate using Siri.

6: Add extra details
Tap the 'Details' section to bring up your iPhone's keyboard. Tap the microphone button in the bottom left, dictate your notes, tap 'Done', and Siri will record what you said in the box.

App used: Dragon Dictation   Price: Free   Difficulty: Beginner   Time needed: 5 minutes

Dictate notes, texts and emails

Give your fingers a rest by dictating notes and text to your iPhone using voice recognition software

 The iPhone's software keyboard has proven a lot more usable than its detractors originally gave it credit for. But there are times when you'd rather not rely on it to create a quick email or post to your Twitter account on the move. Wouldn't it be good to treat your iPhone as your virtual assistant and dictate your message to it? The good news is that you can.

A free voice recognition app, Dragon Dictation, converts your speech into text. A standalone app, its results can be exported easily to the iPhone's Mail app, or shared with any other iPhone app by simple cutting and pasting the text.

If you're thinking that a free app might not produce reliable results, you'd be surprised. Dragon Dictation's voice recognition really is impressive. That's mainly because translation is done remotely: you speak into the app, and it's transmitted to the developer's servers, where it is translated to text and sent back to your iPhone. It sounds a roundabout approach, but it's surprisingly fast and accurate, you just need an internet connection. Here's how to get the most out of spoken text on your iPhone.

Dragon Dictation | Dictate on the iPhone

1: Set up language and settings
Once you've downloaded the app, you'll first have to set up your language and other settings. Dragon Dictation can import your contacts list for easier recognition.

2: Tap to record
Tap the red circle button to record, and speak clearly and naturally into the microphone for anything up to 30 seconds. The red bars indicate your voice level.

3: Analysing your voice
When you are finished, click the red 'Done' button at the bottom and, in a second or two, the words you spoke should appear in the editing screen.

Using voice recognition

Here's the inside scoop on voice-to-text

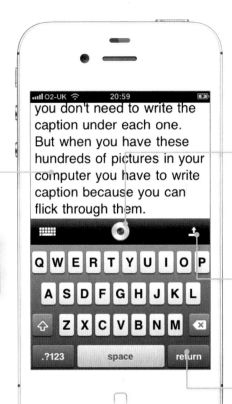

Keep recording
Tap the button to start another voice recognition session. The program can handle up to 30 seconds of text, but you'll get quicker results if you record shorter sessions

Keep it simple
Be careful: the program lacks an autosave feature, so if you quit the app you may lose any text you have been editing here

Transferring text
Tap here to transfer your text to email, text message or social media. You can also adjust settings through this option.

Adding punctuation
Dragon Dictation can understand more than words. If you say 'full stop', 'question mark', or 'new paragraph', for example, the app will understand the context and add the appropriate punctuation to your text.

Using the keyboard
You're not limited to the recognised text. Just as you can with other text editors, you can edit and add your own text using the keyboard

4: Correct errors
If you find any mistakes, you can edit the text by clicking the keyboard button on the left to add or remove text, or even paste text via the iPhone's clipboard.

5: Export the results
Tap the downward arrow button at the bottom right to open up your export options: SMS messaging, email, or the web versions of Facebook and Twitter.

6: Copy and paste
The results are open to just about any app. Tap the Copy button, launch the app you want to add the text to, place the cursor in position and then double-tap.

App used: Pages   Price: £6.99/$9.99   Difficulty: Intermediate   Time needed: 10 minutes

Add your own images to documents in Pages

Want to produce a professional-looking document complete with your favourite pictures? It's easy with Pages

There are plenty of basic text editors available on the iPhone, but when it comes to producing documents that look as though they have been professionally laid out, there's only one choice: Pages.

Apple has taken the desktop power of Pages from the Mac and squeezed it into the iPhone. It lets you easily create documents with the ability to add images directly from your iPhone's Camera Roll, as well as pictures you have synced from iPhoto, making it a fantastic tool for producing excellent results while on the move.

So you could take a picture on the iPhone, edit it with your favourite image editing app and import it into Pages. The superb manipulation features that you can apply to images such as resizing, rotating and moving with your fingers seems much more natural than doing it with a mouse, and can often offer accurate results (although alignment guides are there to help you as you go).

There is also a wide selection of extra effects that you can apply to an image to give it that professional look, including masks to hide part of an image, drop shadows and reflections.

Pages | Add images to documents

1: Grab your photos
Launch Pages and open the document you want to add the image to. Tap 'Media' at the top and in the next window tap the Media tab.

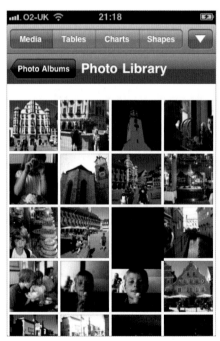

2: Add the image
Navigate to the photo you want from the Camera Roll or Photo Library. When you tap the image it will be added to the document.

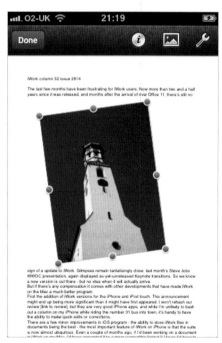

3: Adjust and move
Adjust the size by pinching and dragging the image, move it by tapping and dragging the image, or rotate by pinching and rotating.

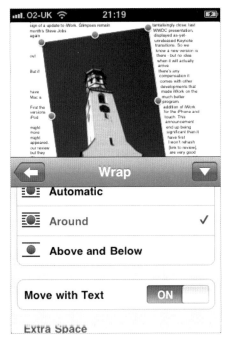

4: Wrap your text

Click the 'i' button. Under the Arrange tab, tap Wrap and choose one of the Wrap options to adjust how the text will flow around the image.

5: Mask things

If you wish to add a mask, select the option and move your finger along the slider to adjust. When you're happy, tap the Mask button.

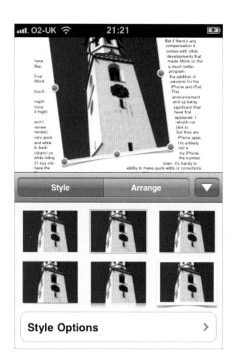

6: Style your image

Apply a style by tapping the Style tab and then tapping one of the six pre-built styles. You can configure an image style with more options.

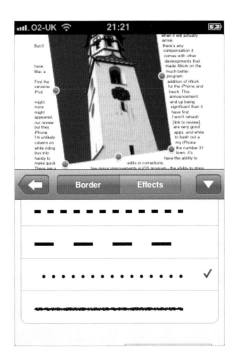

7: Add a border

To add a border to the image, tap the Borders tab in Style Options to set the colour, width and effect of the border you'd like.

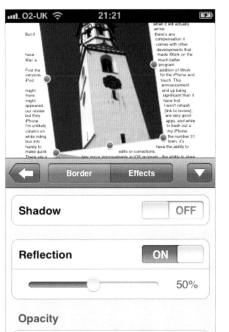

8: Create shadow effects

Tap the Effects tab to add up to three more effects: one of four shadow settings, image reflection and setting the opacity of the image.

9: Complete the edits

Tap the downwards-facing icon to return to page view. You can edit the effects by tapping on the image and clicking the 'i' button.

Productivity

App used: Pages   Price: £6.99/$9.99   Difficulty: Intermediate   Time needed: 5 minutes

Publish your Pages documents to iWork.com

Pages makes it easy to share documents online – and a chosen few can collaborate on documents you share via iWork.com

 Documents created in Pages aren't stuck on your iPhone forever. There are several ways to share them with friends or colleagues. You can email them, sync them to a server or copy them to your desktop computer with iTunes. And did you know that you can also store documents on Apple's iWork.com service and invite others to view them?

iWork.com is a little-used collaboration service for iWork applications, which is currently free and in beta. However, it's a surprisingly powerful service. On the iWork.com website, document collaborators can view pixel-perfect previews of your document, and make notes and comments, even simultaneously.

One of the best reasons for sharing your work on iWork.com is that the results are platform agnostic. That means that you can collaborate just as easily with PC users as your Mac friends. In fact, anyone with a web browser can view your files, and those you're sharing the document with can download the file in Microsoft Office and PDF formats, as well as a native Pages file – all with your permission, of course. iWork.com isn't perfect, but it's a great way of sharing your work.

Pages | Sharing a document in Pages

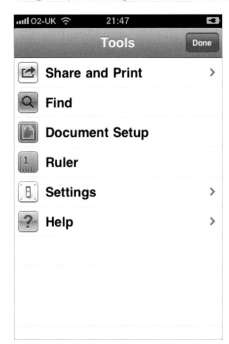

1: Complete the document
When you have finished editing the file you want to share with others, tap the Settings icon found at the top of the document – it looks like a spanner.

2: Hit the share menu
Tap Share and Print and then select Share via iWork.com. You'll have to sign in using your Apple ID and password before you can share any of your files.

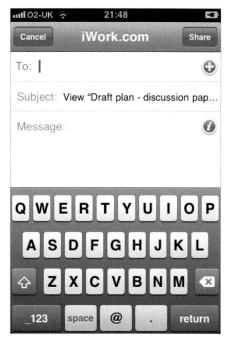

3: Chose recipients
Mail will open, and an email has been created with the subject line filled in. Enter the email address of anyone you wish to share the document with.

Setting up a shared file

The many ways you can share a Pages file

● **Share any document**
Want to share another document? Tap the document name and you can choose from any of the other documents you've uploaded in the past

● **Password protection**
Concerned about security? You can password-protect the shared document to be absolutely sure only your collaborators see it'

Getting started on iWork.com
While you need an Apple ID and password to set up an account at iWork.com, those you're collaborating with don't. They just click the link emailed to them and it should open in a browser, irrespective of the platform they're using.

● **Commenting**
You can comment on shared documents by default, but you can turn this option off if you'd rather keep things clutter-free

● **PDF, Pages or Word?**
Leaving this option unchecked allows the people you're collaborating with to download the file from iWork.com in any one of three formats

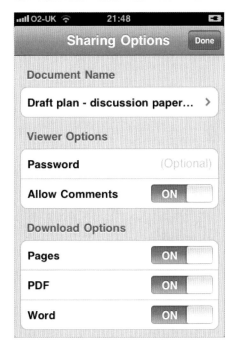

4: Adjust the options
Tap the 'i' icon to set various options, including whether to allow comments on the document and whether viewers can download it. Now just click Done.

5: Watch the progress
Click the Share button and a progress bar shows the upload process. Click the Done button when finished – all users will receive a notification email.

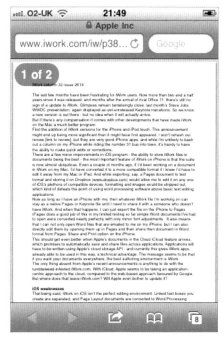

6: View the shared document
Viewers who click the link in the email they receive can now see the file on iWork.com in their web browser. It even works on the mobile version of Safari.

App used: Keynote   Price: £6.99/$8.99   Difficulty: Intermediate   Time needed: 15 minutes

Create a Keynote presentation

How to get started with Keynote and create slides that will grab the attention of your colleagues

 Designed exclusively for the iPhone, iPad and iPod touch, Keynote (Apple, £6.99/$8.99) makes creating attention-grabbing presentations – complete with animated charts and transitions – as easy as tapping the screen and dragging a few objects around.

When starting out with the app you can choose from 12 pre-designed themes or simply dive in and create your own slides from scratch,

which is unbelievably easy. You just tap the screen to start adding text and then import images from your Photo Album, which you can drag into position, resize, rotate and mask to make your slides look amazing. You have complete freedom to create and edit your slides however you see fit and the panel to the side of the screen lets you drag them into order ready for when you come to present them to others. The app even integrates your Notes app, so you

can add your own cue cards and informative nuggets to read out when you are presenting your slides to other people.

In this tutorial we guide you through the basics of creating your own Keynote presentation. However, the more you experiment with this app the more proficient you will get at using its intuitive interface and having fun creating slides that will enthral and amaze your friends and colleagues.

Using Keynote
Create captivating presentations

● **Add some style**
The 'i' icon is essentially a style icon with options to tailor whatever object you currently have highlighted, such as images or text

● **Add images**
Tap on the picture icon to add images. You can then press and hold to position them and double-tap them to apply masking effects

● **Re-arranging your slides**
All of your created slides will appear in sequence in the panel to the left. If you press and hold on a slide then you can drag it and move it up or down to re-arrange the order. You can add extra slides to your sequence by tapping on the '+' icon at the bottom of the column.

● **Options menu**
The spanner icon is the options menu that allows you access to 'Settings', 'Help', 'Find', plus all of the various options for sharing your work

● **Animate your work**
Tap on the spanner icon and choose 'Animation Mode' to apply animations to your slides, such as the transitional effects between two images

Keynote | Create your first presentation

1: Start creating
When you first launch Keynote, read the tutorial slides as these are a great introduction to just how easy it is to use the app. When you're ready, tap the '+' icon to create a new slide.

2: Choose a theme
Keynote comes pre-loaded with 12 themes to help you get started on your presentation slides. When starting out it is a good idea to use one as a template for your own work.

3: Add images
Pictures from your Photo Album can be imported into Keynote by tapping on the picture icon on the top bar. Scroll through your album and then tap an image to import.

4: Mask your images
Once your image is in position, double-tap on it to bring up the 'masking' options. Use the slider to apply a mask to your image (scaling within its picture box).

5: Add text
Text can be written straight onto the page, then dragged around the screen and positioned where you want – the templates aren't set in stone, so do with them what you will.

6: Apply some style
If you tap the 'i' icon on the top bar you can apply style to whatever is selected (text or images). Tapping this icon with text highlighted will allow you to bold it, italicise it or underline it.

7: Add animations
When you have a series of slides prepared, tap the spanner icon and choose 'Animation Mode'. This lets you determine the effect as you cycle through slides.

8: Choose effects
Choose a slide from your list and then pick an effect from the menu provided – this will then provide an eye-catching transition between your slides. You can pick one for each slide.

9: Make some notes
To ensure your presentations run smoothly, you can also add notes, such as facts and cue cards to help when you come to present your slides to others.

App used: Numbers **Price:** £6.99/$9.99 **Difficulty:** Intermediate **Time needed:** 15 minutes

Create a useful spreadsheet in Numbers

Use Numbers on the iPhone to create everyday spreadsheets

There's a lot of uses for Numbers on the iPhone beyond working on your spreadsheets away from the office. With some clever use of formulas you can create documents to help you with everyday tasks such as planning a monthly budget. What's more, if you're updated to iOS 5 and connected to iCloud, your documents will be backed up and synced, ready for editing on your Mac or other iOS devices.

In this tutorial, you'll create a simple but incredibly useful shopping list spreadsheet. As well as presenting groceries in a logical order,

you can input prices of each item. Finally, it'll allow you to tick items off as you put them in your trolley. This isn't the only use of Numbers on your iPhone, but it's certainly a great example of one of its features. If you've used Numbers on a Mac, you'll find the interface familiar and you'll have no trouble diving straight in and creating spreadsheets. That said, if you're new to editing documents in Numbers then you'll have no trouble getting to grips with things, just follow the simple steps in this tutorial and you'll be well on your way to creating great spreadsheets on the go.

Numbers | Create a shopping spreadsheet

1: Choose a template
Numbers has ready-made templates that can be edited to your needs. For this example, fire up the app and choose the Checklist template, as this is closest to a shopping list.

2: Add a title
Double-tap on the original checklist title to edit it and this will bring up your iPhone's keyboard. Delete the old title and give it a new, more relevant one such as, 'My Shopping List'.

3: Change your headers
Double-tap on each of the table's column headers and edit their names. When you're happy with your new title, tap the green tick icon in the top-right of your screen to confirm.

Mastering Numbers

A closer look at the Numbers interface

Changing the format
Changing the format of any cell is as easy as tapping the icons underneath the input box. The numbers format is displayed as the number 42

Formats explained
There are plenty of cell formats to choose from depending on the nature of your spreadsheet, they include time/date, complex equations, text, and currency

Check it off
When you're happy with what you've added to a cell, simply tap the green tick icon in the top-right corner to confirm and save

Drag and pinch
To navigate your way around a spreadsheet, simply drag it and use the pinch gestures to zoom in and out, much like a photo

Sync and share with iCloud
If you've updated your iPhone to iOS 5, you'll have no doubt noticed a feature called iCloud. If you sign up for a free iCloud account you'll be able to store, back up and sync your Numbers spreadsheets across all of your iOS 5 devices and your Mac (so long as it runs OS X Lion 10.7.2 or later).

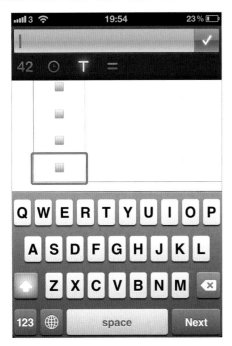

4: Fix the format
Scroll to the bottom of the spreadsheet and double-tap the bottom tick-box in the left column. Delete it using the backspace key on the keyboard and type in 'Total'.

5: Total it up
Double-tap the cell next to the Total label, select the equals sign at the top so it turns blue, then tap the SUM button. This should automatically add up the shopping list prices above.

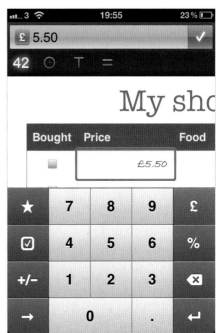

6: Add some details
To add shopping list items double-tap on cells and type them in. For item prices you'll need to tap the '£' sign to ensure that they're formatted and totalled up correctly.

App used: Dropbox Price: Free Difficulty: Beginner Time needed: 15 minutes

Transfer files using Dropbox

How to transfer files wirelessly between computer and iPhone

To get the maximum use out of your iPhone, using it as a portable workstation and working remotely outside of the office has got to be one of the premier attractions. There are plenty of apps that allow you to transfer your files back to your computer wirelessly, but few are as intuitive as Dropbox has proved to be.

Dropbox is a free app from Dropbox Inc and, when used in tandem with the free Dropbox desktop software (which you can get for Mac or PC from **www.dropbox.com**), you can copy files into your desktop Dropbox and, within a few seconds, be able to view and access them

on your iPhone. It's a two-way process, so any alterations you make on your iPhone will then be applied to the versions in your desktop Dropbox thanks to quick-fire syncing. It's a wondrous tool that is easy to set up and use and, best of all, the amount of cloud storage space is a whopping 2.2GB, meaning that you can copy a bulk of files into your Dropbox, either from your computer or your iPhone and they will be stored in your 'cloud'.

In this tutorial we guide you through the process of setting up your own Dropbox and showcase some of the great features that this app provides.

Dropbox | Transfer files wirelessly

1: Launch the app
Download the free app and then launch it on your iPhone. You will also need to download the free software for your home computer from **www.dropbox.com**.

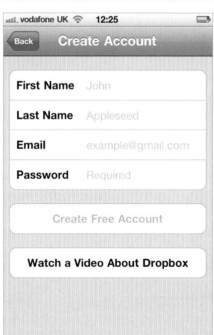

2: Create an account
Choose the 'I'm new to Dropbox' option at the main menu and then input all the required details to create a new free account. You can then read an intro to the app.

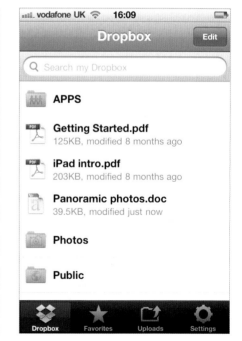

3: Sync and transfer
As long as you enter the same login details for both the app and the desktop version of Dropbox then all folders and files copied to your Dropbox will be automatically synced.

Why Dropbox is the easy option

Transferring your files using Dropbox is a quick and easy process that takes just a few seconds

● Dropbox
The 'Dropbox' section provides a list of all of the folders and files currently occupying your Dropbox. These are automatically synced between your iPhone and computer

● Favourites
By viewing files within Dropbox and marking them as favourites, those particular files will be automatically downloaded for you to access offline

● Settings
If you need additional help with using the Dropbox app, or want to check various others settings then simply tap the 'Settings' icon

● Uploads
The 'Uploads' option allows you to transfer images from your iPhone to your computer, but first you have to give the app authorisation to access Photos

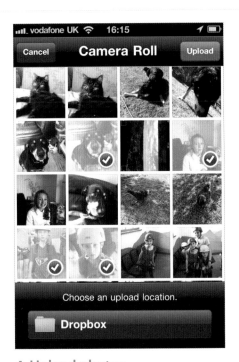

4: Upload photos
To transfer photos from iPhone to computer tap 'Uploads' and press '+'. Authorise access to your photos, ensure your Location Services are on choose images and press 'Upload'.

5: Add favourites
View files in the Dropbox app and tap the star icon to mark that file as a favourite. It will automatically download for you to access, even if you aren't connected to the internet.

6: View settings
Tap the 'Settings' icon to access information, such as the version of the app you are running, remaining cloud space, apply a password and additional help.

Entertainment
Read, watch and listen on the move

128 Make and manage your own playlists using the music-streaming service Spotify

130 Use your iPhone as a Scrabble tile rack in order to keep your letters more private

132 Use your own photos to create comic strips

138 Bookmark your favourite pages in Kindle

140 Subscribe to your favourite magazines

142 Be in the competition with Game Center

"Listen to music, read books and play games on the iPhone"

Difficulty: Beginner   Time needed: 5 minutes

Customise the Music dock

There is a limited amount of space to display options in the Music dock; we show you how to tailor it to your needs

We sincerely love our old iPods, but now you can ferry your entire music collection around with you, as well as your contacts, calendars and everything else your iPhone allows.

The Music app on your iPhone (previously iPod prior to iOS 5) is wonderfully versatile and allows you to play music, audiobooks and podcasts downloaded from your iPhone's iTunes app without having to go through the hassle of syncing to a computer, but did you know that you can customise the interface to suit your own specific needs?

When you launch the app you will be presented with a series of categories at the

bottom of the screen that allow you to fast-track to the items that really matter to you. However, what if you prefer audiobooks to albums? The More category will allow you to access all of the categories that aren't immediately accessible from the Music app's dock, and by pressing the Edit button it is possible to chop and change the categories that are presented in your dock to the ones you will access and use the most.

It's a quick and easy process that only takes a few minutes and in this tutorial we will guide you through the simple steps to personalising your Music dock to meet your own requirements.

Music | Customising your Music dock

1: Launch the app
First launch your Music app. This can be found in the dock at the bottom of your Home screen, although you can tap and hold the icon to drag it out into another position.

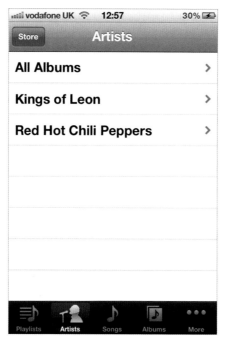

2: Go to the dock
Observe the dock at the bottom of the screen; by default this will contain five options: Playlists, Artists, Songs, Albums and More. For the purpose of this exercise, tap the More option.

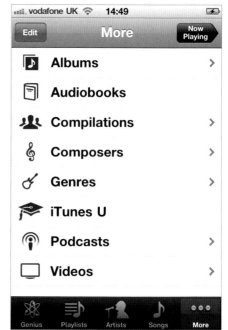

3: Add to the dock
The app now displays more options: Albums, Audiobooks, Compilations, Composers, Genres, etc. These are categories that you can add to your dock to replace the existing ones.

Organise your Music app

Personalise your Music dock by mixing up the content categories

Your content
Tapping on a category in your dock will list all content in that category, allowing you to find what you want quickly

Your dock
Your Music dock allows you to quickly access four categories, you can decide which ones and change the order of the ones presented

Now Playing
If you currently have content playing on your Music, whether it's active or paused, you can tap the 'Now Playing' button to find out what it is

New order
You don't have to replace the categories in your dock through this process, you can simply change the order of the existing ones if you prefer. To do this, tap and hold the icon you wish to move and then drag it over the position you would prefer it to go to and the switch will take place immediately.

More categories
If you tap the More option then all of the remaining categories will be presented in a list. Tap Edit to change what appears in your dock

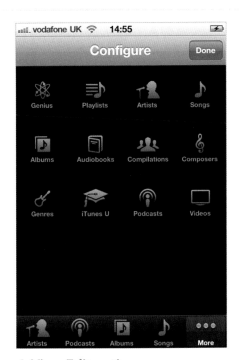

4: View Edit options
While on the page of extra options, tap Edit and all possible options will then be displayed on a single screen. Now you can start editing what appears in your dock.

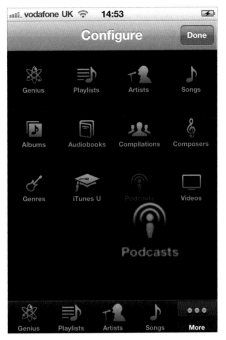

5: Drag to replace
To replace an existing category in your dock, simply press and hold on the option you want and then drag it to the dock over the category that you'd like to replace, then release it.

6: Set your categories
When you are happy tap the Done button in the top-right corner and your categories will be set. Of course, you can go back to edit them at any time by repeating the process.

App used: Spotify   Price: Free   Difficulty: Beginner   Time needed: 5 minutes

Make and manage playlists in Spotify

Spotify takes on a whole new dimension on your phone

When Spotify first launched, it offered a pretty generous service, with free streaming interspersed with adverts, or advert-free streaming supported by a monthly fee. In the increasingly competitive music market, it has had to restrict some other services developed since the launch to subscribers only, including the ability to listen to your music over a 3G connection, and also to make music that you don't have a physical copy of available for offline listening. The exact combinations of what you can and can't do with a free account are a bit fiddly, and explained in some detail on Spotify's website, but there's a seven-day free trial of the Premium service, so you can compare the two for yourself first hand.

The app itself is slick, and provides access to all manner of content thanks to the Search function. Obviously this is quicker over Wi-Fi, but also works over a cellular data connection. When you have the Spotify software on your computer, you can sync music from iTunes to the phone, and also manage playlists on the go from your computer and phone. These playlists are stored remotely, so whenever you log in to your Spotify account on a device, they will be available for you to listen to.

Spotify | Manage and stream music

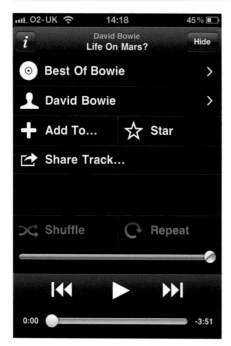

1: Search for tracks
Look for a track using the Search function. Click on it to play it, then tap the screen to call up the menu. Choose 'Add To Playlist', and then give the playlist a name on the following screen.

2: Add further tracks
You can search for tracks by the same artist, and add them using the same technique. Add tracks from your library by connecting your phone to the Spotify software on your Mac.

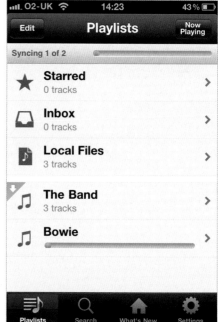

3: Listen offline
With a Premium account, you can listen to tracks when you have no internet connection. Click on the playlist, and select Available Offline >Yes. The tracks will be synced to your iPhone.

Connecting your iPhone with Spotify

Your iPhone can read your iTunes library – even when you're out of the house

My devices
Manage the devices that are connected to your Spotify account here. Playlists that you create and edit are synced automatically across devices

Premium account
To enable offline listening of some types of content, you will need a Premium account, which also gets rid of the adverts

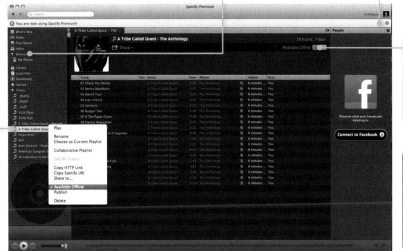

Offline listening
Playlists on any device can be made available offline with a Premium account, meaning that they will be available without you having to access any kind of network

Manage playlists
Playlists can be managed and renamed both on your computer and on your iPhone. You can filter content to quickly create playlists

Sharing Spotify
There are also sharing options on Spotify, such as sending tracks you like to Last.fm and Facebook, so you can keep friends in the loop about your current favourite songs and artists.

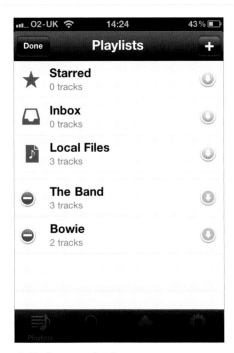

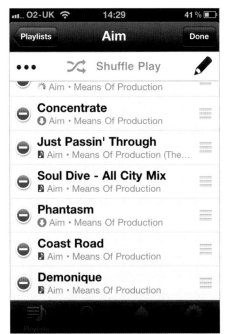

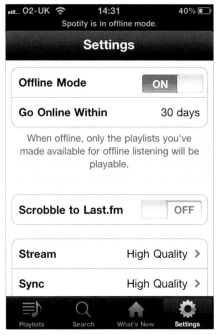

4: Delete a playlist
In the Playlists menu, click 'Edit', and delete buttons appear. The green circles denote that a playlist is available for offline listening. Tap one to make them unavailable for offline listening.

5: Edit a playlist
Click on the pencil icon, and you can edit the playlist. Use the red icons to delete a track or pick tracks up by their right hand edge, and drag them to re-order them.

6: Go offline
This requires a Premium account. Go into the Settings menu and switch Spotify offline. This means that only the playlists you have chosen to make available offline will be playable.

Keep your Scrabble letters private

Pair your iPhone with your iPad and use it as a Scrabble tile rack with the full iPad game

App used: SCRABBLE™
Tile Rack

Price: Free

Difficulty: Beginners

Time taken: 2 minutes

Scrabble is a popular traditional board game now available on many mobile devices. It is a simple word-based board game that relies on privacy of each player's game pieces. A main component of the game is for players to have a rack of tiles that each contain a single letter. These tiles are kept private so that other players won't know what opponents are able to play, thus maintaining the competitive nature of the game.

With the arrival of the iPad, Scrabble is now a popular game to play on the tablet device. It is large enough to display the Scrabble game board and allows multiple players to interact with the game. Although the iPad can be used as a multiplayer device, it is difficult for users to keep their letter tiles private, therefore compromising the integrity of the game.

With this in mind, an app has been developed to use in conjunction with the iPad to further enhance the game experience. SCRABBLE™ Tile Rack is a separate application for the iPhone that is designed to be paired with an iPad and used as individual tile racks.

The iPad app allows up to four iPhones to be connected through a Bluetooth connection, giving each player a wireless connection to the game board. Using the iPhone application is very simple, allowing users to control both their game tiles and the iPad-based game board from the application.

Getting to know the tile rack

A look at how the SCRABBLE™ Tile Rack works

● **Search for words**
Built in to the application is a simple dictionary. Pressing this button brings up a new window that allows you to verify whether specific words are allowed

● **Shuffle and swap**
Shuffling or swapping your tiles can be easily done from the buttons on this main screen. This allows you to adjust your playing tiles without other players seeing

● **Rotate the app**
The Rotate button allows you to remotely control the orientation of the application on the iPad. By pressing it, the iPad screen will rotate 90 degrees, and can therefore be adjusted for each player when it is their turn

● **Recall your tiles**
Once tiles have been placed onto the iPad screen, you may wish to change your mind, or correct a mistake. Simply pressing the Recall button will return all of the tiles back to your tile rack

Wi-Fi
Your Wi-Fi connection can sometimes hinder the connection of the Bluetooth of both devices. Ensuring this setting is switched off before the applications are launched will allow the devices to sync quickly and maintain a strong connection.

SCRABBLE™ Tile Rack | Using the tile rack

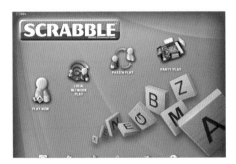

1: Get the iPad app

To begin using the tile rack, you will first need to have the iPad application available. Ensure that the Bluetooth setting is switched on and then start up the Scrabble application on the iPad.

2: Select Party Play

Using the tile rack can only be done within a multiplayer 'Party Play' game, which can be selected from the iPad app's main screen. Clicking on this icon will then prompt you to connect your iPhone.

3: Connect the iPhone

Before starting the SCRABBLE™ Tile Rack application, ensure the iPhone's Bluetooth setting is turned on, but the Wi-Fi setting is turned off. This will allow the iPhone and iPad to connect smoothly.

4: Connect to the game

Once the iPhone application has been launched, there will be a prompt to seek local games of Scrabble. More than one player will need to be connected to the game before it can start.

5: View the main screen

The main tile rack screen will be presented once the game has started. From this screen you are then able to control most of the components of the game that are being played on the iPad.

6: Play your tiles

When it is your turn to play, a prompt will appear on the iPhone screen. To play your tiles, drag the ones you want and drop them on the Scrabble board above. This places them in the relevant slots on the iPad.

7: Recall tiles

If you change your mind, or have made a mistake, simply press the Recall button on your iPhone. This will bring all of the tiles you have played back to your tile rack, and off the iPad screen.

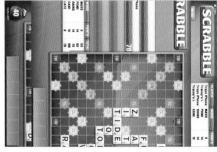

8: Rotate the screen

With multiple users, it is likely the iPad will not be facing the correct direction for each player. The Rotate button on the iPhone interface allows players to turn the iPad screen without physically moving it.

9: Play the game

The game board is displayed on the iPad, and is viewable to all players. Once tiles have been placed on the game board, pressing the green tick will confirm the move, completing your turn and moving play on.

App used: Strip Designer **Price:** £1.99/$2.99 **Difficulty:** Beginner **Time taken:** 20 minutes

Turn day trips into comic strips with Strip Designer

Give your photos from that day trip a bit of extra sparkle

While every photo might say a thousand words, sometimes it's nice to be able to actually add some of your own, and now, thanks to Strip Designer on your iPhone, it is possible to do so.

The app allows you to upload your photos and turn them into a comic strip, giving you control of their look and exactly what they say by giving you the chance to insert speech bubbles and action stickers to really make them stand out. You can then easily export your creations to your social networks for all your friends to see exactly what that trip to the beach was like.

Strip Designer relies on touch screen gestures to allow you to express yourself, altering the angle of photos, as well as the zoom and visual effects. Images can be uploaded from your iPhone's photo library or alternatively imported from your Facebook account in-app. It's a smooth process from start to finish and, although the editing gestures do take some getting used to, it won't be long before you're dropping in 'Pow!' stickers and thought bubbles with ease. So dig out those day-trip photos, create your own fun adventures, and share them with your friends and family.

Strip Designer | Create your comic strip

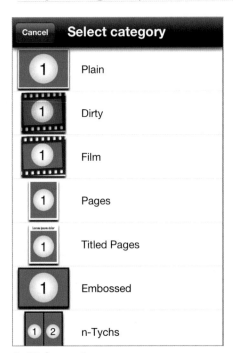

1: Pick a strip
Upon entering the app, tap the Create New icon to get started on your comic book. The first thing you need to do is pick a page layout for your page.

2: Add photos
Once you have chosen your design, you will see each frame of the page contains the message 'Add Photo'. Tap each one and then select an image.

3: Shape photos
You can use screen gestures to change the angle of your images on the page. Pinch to zoom, tap on an image, and you can then tilt or resize the photo.

Your comic strip hub

How to bring your photos to life

● Share
The envelope icon is the base for sending out your comic strips to the world. You can post them to Facebook or Flickr, as well as AirPrint your designs

● My comics
The in-app library of all your various projects, this icon takes you back to the home screen of the app from where you can manage your strips

● Page
Add a new page by tapping the Page icon and selecting a layout for those on offer. You can add unlimited numbers of pages to a project

Share settings
Before you share your comic strip, you can edit the export settings of your file, setting the image to high resolution if you wish, as well as altering the image format. You have the choice to export as a jpeg or a png file.

● Add
From this tab you can select and drop in comic-strip features like action stickers and thought bubbles to give your images some dialogue and more of a story

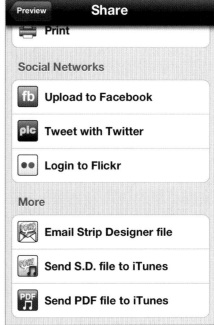

4: Add image effects
To get the comic-book feel, you can add effects to your images, including things like halftone. Use the on-screen scroll bar to set the strength of the edit.

5: Give it a comic style
The real comic-book features can by found by tapping the Add icon that's in the menu bar. This option contains comic stickers as well as speech bubbles.

6: Share your creation
Once you have completed your creation, you can then share it with the world via the Share icon. Your strip will be rendered before showing you a preview.

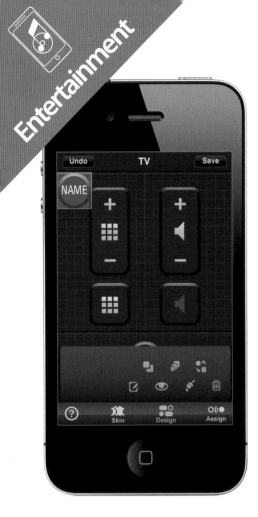

App used: L5 Remote **Price:** Free **Difficulty:** Intermediate **Time needed:** 10 minutes

Turn your iPhone into a universal remote control

Having more than one remote is so last century. This funky accessory will enhance your channel-changing life

It's a little irksome that the iPhone doesn't ship with any kind of infrared controller, as it would be great to use the device as a universal remote for our televisions, Blu-ray players and satellite receivers. Luckily, this missed opportunity by Apple has been seized upon by L5. It has created a tiny dongle and app that can do the job, turning your iPhone into an easy-to-use remote that can control anything with an infrared beam.

What's more, the set-up process is really straightforward, so you don't need to spend hours scanning through infrared wavelengths. Simply make sure that all the buttons you want are covered and then sit back and enjoy controlling your digital world. If you have a mischievous side, you could neglect to inform a partner that you have enabled your iPhone as a remote control and torture them by constantly changing channel during their favourite show, though we take no responsibility for such behaviour! In this step by step, we'll teach you how to set up the remote once you've bought the dongle and plugged it into the connector at the bottom of your iPhone.

L5 Remote | Combine every remote into one app

1: Choose a template
Here you can decide whether to use a template for your remote or custom build one. We suggest opting for a Quick remote if you are new to the app.

2: Button up
Follow the prompt and tap on the first button you want to assign. Volume is a good starting point. It's a good idea to have your TV remote ready to go.

3: Press 'em
Press on the volume up button on your TV remote and the L5 will cleverly detect the signal and then copy it so that it can use it on your own TV.

Create a universal remote control
Make your channel-surfing life much easier

Remote access
This number at the bottom indicates how many remotes you have set up, and tapping it will take you to the edit screen where you can add, remove and rename your remotes

Sync
You can set up an account with L5 to sync your settings across multiple devices. This way, you can add the same remotes to everyone's iOS device

Help
Tap the question mark to access the help section. It's very easy to use and it will answer any questions you have about setting up a remote

Advanced settings
Aside from the everyday button pressing, you can also add advanced functions like macros to your remote. These macros will initiate a string of commands like turning on multiple devices, changing channels and setting volumes levels, all from one button press. See the L5 website for more details.

Using the cogs
You can use this button to customise your remote. Just drag and drop buttons onto the grid that appears in the window above

4: View the status
As you add each button to the L5 Remote app you will see status bars appear, which let you know that the app is working and that the hardware is too.

5: Name it
As you can add multiple remotes, you now need to name the one you've created. Tap the number 1 at the bottom of the screen and then the Edit button.

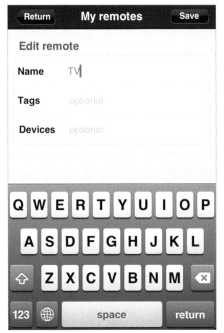

6: Make it easy
Give your remote the easiest name possible so that you'll never get confused. You can now add as many as you like and name them all differently.

App used: Kindle   Price: Free   Difficulty: Biginner   Time needed: 5 minutes

Download and read eBooks using Kindle

Build up a library of books on your iPhone's Kindle app, so you can read your favourite authors on the go

 Before eReaders were invented, we had to lug our holiday reading around on slabs of dead tree. Printed books took up valuable space in our suitcase, and no matter how much you love the feel of a solid product in your hands, they were often very inconvenient.

In these digital days, the Kindle app provides a much more convenient way of storing our holiday or day-to-day reading. As well as enabling us to read electronic books (or eBooks) on the iPhone's screen, we can use Kindle to shop for them as well. This saves us the hassle of popping out to the high street bookshop or having to anxiously wait for the postman to deliver books in time for our holiday's departure date. Instead this can all be done in just a few clicks, plus there are a wealth of free books available to download, including some of the all-time classics.

Kindle was initially just a tablet from Amazon that enabled book lovers to read digital copies. However, iPhone owners can download the free Kindle app and turn their iPhone into a reader with ease, saving them the expense of buying a dedicated digital book reader.

Kindle | Learn how to get eBooks onto your iPhone

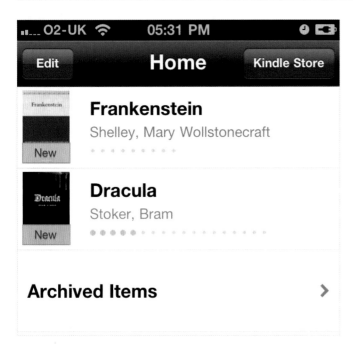

1: Open Kindle
Download the Kindle app from the App Store and install it on your iPhone. Tapping on the Kindle icon takes you to the Home screen. This is where your books will be stored. To find some reading material, click on the 'Kindle Store' button at the top right.

2: Go shopping
The Kindle eBook store is part of the Amazon website, so there are plenty of books to choose from. Peruse one of the featured new books on the Kindle Store's homepage, or browse through your favourite categories by clicking on a link. Like iBooks, Amazon offers some free popular classics.

Interact with a Kindle eBook

Discover the extra bells and whistles you get from an eBook

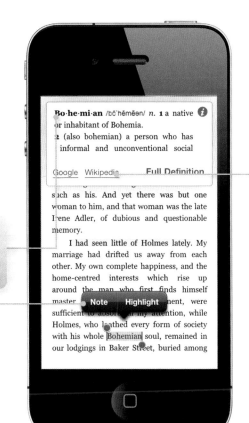

Dictionary
Not sure of what a word means? Hold down on it to highlight it and a dictionary definition will appear at the top of the screen

Notes and highlight
To help you find a particular bit of text at a later date, hold your finger down on it and drag to make a selection. You can then type in a note or select a highlight colour

Explore further
The Wikipedia link will take you to the related Wikipedia page, giving you a history of the selected letter. The Google link takes you to Google search results

Fabulous freebies
As well as downloading sample chapters from many new eBooks, you can download entire books for free using the Kindle eBook reader. This is a great way to catch up with the classics of literature. Simply tap on the link to the online Kindle store to launch it in Safari, then scroll down to the Free Popular Classics section. You can then browse through thousands of books and enjoy adventure tales featuring Conan Doyle's *Sherlock Holmes*, or chill your spine with the work of HP Lovecraft.

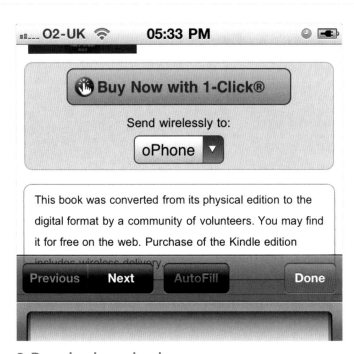

3: Download your book
Tap on a thumbnail to discover more about a book, and read customer reviews to help you make an informed choice. If you fancy buying the book tap the 'Buy now with 1-click' button. Alternatively, download a free sample chapter. Make sure you set it to deliver to your iPhone.

4: Start reading
To read a downloaded book, tap on its cover in your Kindle Home screen. Turn pages by tapping the screen or swiping left or right. You can bookmark a page by tapping the middle of the screen and then tapping the '+' button at the bottom.

App used: Kindle   **Price:** Free   **Difficulty:** Beginner   **Time needed:** 2 minutes

Bookmark your pages in Kindle

With Amazon's free eBook reader, you'll never lose your place in an epic read again. Learn how to add your own bookmarks

Many of us have already discovered how easy it is to read books on the iPhone – they are more portable than your average paperback, and can store huge quantities of literature. As you use eBook reader apps such as iBooks and Kindle more regularly, more features and quirks will become apparent to convince you that you need never return to the printed page ever again.

Bookmarking the pages of a printed book is easy, as you can fashion a placeholder out of anything. With Kindle you can store multiple bookmarks to ensure that you need never run the risk of losing your page again. You can also add your own notes and highlight key words and phrases, plus you can download an in-app dictionary to enlighten you on the definitions of any new words that you come across. And we haven't even touched on the other additional information you can access to gain a better understanding of the book, the characters and the settings! In this tutorial we guide you through the simple process of bookmarking the pages of a downloaded Kindle eBook.

Kindle | Bookmarking your favourite reads

1: Open a book
Any books that you have downloaded through Amazon will appear in your own archive. Simply select a book that you would like to read and then tap the cover to open it.

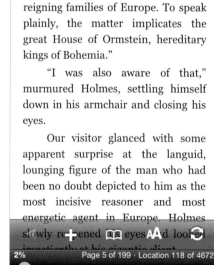

2: Add a bookmark
When you get to a point at which you have to stop reading, tap the page to bring up the interface options and then tap the '+' symbol to bookmark your current page.

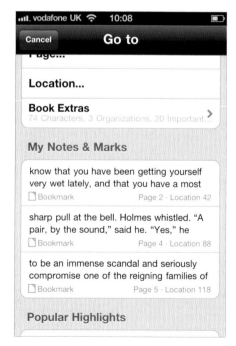

3: Access your bookmarks
When you return to your book, you can tap on the open book icon to access your bookmarks, that appear under 'My Notes & Marks' along with an excerpt of text and a page number.

Making your mark

Thanks to an intuitive interface, you'll never lose your place in a Kindle book

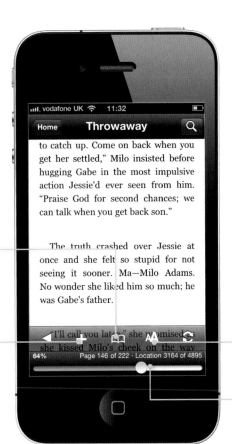

Changing the appearance
You can change the text font, size and colour by tapping this icon, tailoring the appearance of the pages to suit your needs

Accessing bookmarks
When you want to jump to one of your bookmarked pages, tap the open book icon and then tap on a bookmark from your list

Optional extras
Most books that you download come with information that can be accessed by tapping the book icon while on a page and then selecting 'Book Extras'. Here you may be able to access info on characters and places in the book, as well as find out when it was first published and how many books there are in the series.

Adding bookmarks
When you arrive at a page you would like to bookmark, tap the page to bring up the options and then tap the '+' icon

Page slider
If you simply want to skip to a good bit of a book, you can use the slider at the bottom of the screen rather than turning each page individually

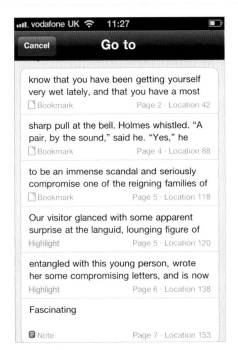

4: Instantly access
To access a bookmark, browse through your list – if you have multiple bookmarks saved – and then tap on one of your bookmarks to instantly jump to a particular page.

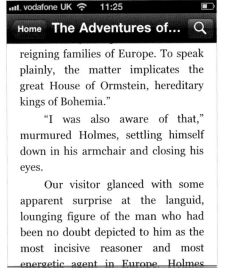

5: Delete a bookmark
To remove a bookmark from your list tap on it to select it from your list and then you will be taken to the page, then tap the page to bring up the interface options and then press the '–' symbol.

6: Highlight and make notes
It is possible to highlight words or paragraphs and add notes. While on a page, press and hold over a word and drag to highlight sections, then choose Highlight or Note from the options.

Difficulty: Beginner **Time needed:** 20 minutes

Set up a subscription on Newsstand

The built-in app allows you to subscribe to your favourite magazines and get the new issue on release day without lifting a finger. Here's how…

 The release of iOS 5 brought with it a range of new features to make life with your iPhone or iPad easier, such as keeping on top of all your favourite reading using Newsstand. The excitement for Newsstand stems from the fact that it means new developers have started fresh on their mobile publications, learning from previous mistakes to provide a better reading experience for iOS 5 users. The other big positive with Newsstand is that you can set up subscriptions to your favourite magazines, so you never miss an issue.

More and more magazines are becoming available via Newsstand and the App Store, meaning the amount of choice you have is growing constantly, each trying to stand out from the crowd with interactive features and extra content. Setting up a subscription is a simple process and a very good way to get your bearings in the App Store should you be new to iOS.

Newsstand | Download a magazine subscription

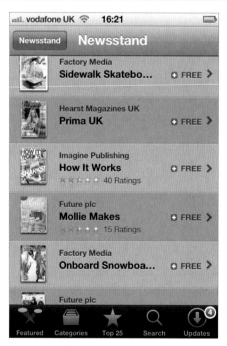

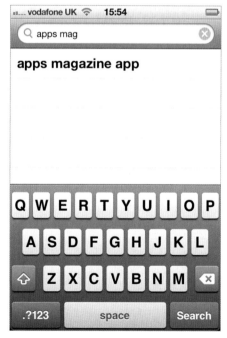

1: Open Newsstand
On your Home screen, tap the Newsstand icon to open up the app and see your current library of magazine titles. This is where all your downloaded items are displayed.

2: Visit the Store
To start your magazine search, tap the Store button at the top of the display. This will take you to the Newsstand wing of the App Store where you can search for digital publications.

3: Search
Here you can browse through all the magazines on sale either using the various breakdowns provided by the Store, or tapping Featured and then using the search bar.

Making sense of Newsstand

Find your way around this magazine archive

Info

When you find a magazine for you, don't just tap Install, instead tap the icon and get the extra info, including reviews and cost of each issue

Auto subscriptions

Always keep track of your subscriptions as some automatically renew without you physically tapping to do so. Make a note if a title you download tells you this, which it will do, so you don't get a nasty surprise when you get your bank statement six months after you thought a subscription has ended.

Featured titles

At the top of this page is the animated Featured window, where a selection of the most popular titles are displayed, and is a good place to start your browsing

Menu tabs

Along the bottom of the screen you have various tabs to help you navigate, including charts of the best apps as well as Genius, which offers you download suggestions

Search

If you tap the Search tab at the bottom of the page, you'll be able to search for all Newsstand compatible publications

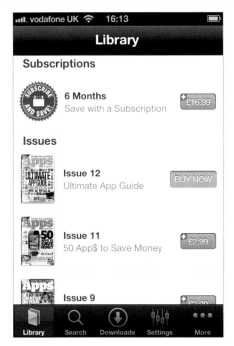

4: Install

Once you've found the title you were looking for, tap Install and enter your iTunes password to download it to your library, where you can access back issues and set up that subscription.

5: Subscribe

It may take a few minutes to download, but once it has, tap the cover to enter its personal library, and tap the subscribe icon to see what options are on offer before purchasing.

6: Read

Once you've chosen your subscription and entered your password, the latest issue will become available in the magazine's library. Tap it to download, and start reading.

Difficulty: Beginner   Time needed: 10 minutes

Get more out of Game Center

Explore your iOS gaming hub and discover how to get games, find friends and beat your mates in online multiplayer

PSN, Xbox Live, all the leading games consoles have dedicated online channels for you to find friends, chat and engage in some online multiplayer action – and your iPhone is no different. Game Center is your iOS gaming hub and through it you can set up a gaming profile, search and discover the latest games and find friends to compete against.

Finding your way around Game Center is easy and, once your profile has been set up, you can get to work earning high scores with which to compete against other players all over the world. You can search for games all from within your Game Center app, which also means that you only install games that are compatible with the service. You can still install games by browsing through the App Store, but be sure to look out for the Game Center logo for compatibility. When you have compiled a friends list then you can compare scores and play against each other in games that support two-players. In this tutorial we guide you around Game Center.

Game Center | Finding your way around your gaming hub

1: Set your status
Adding a status to your Game Center allows you to apply some personality to your profile. Tap the text box in the middle of the screen and then enter a message of intent.

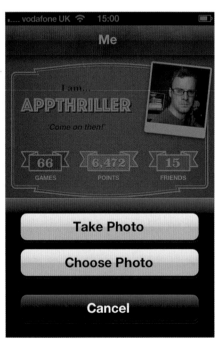

2: Add a photo
You can assign a photo to your profile by either tapping on the photo frame or selecting the 'Change Photo' option. Choose an image from your Camera Roll to assign.

3: Find friends
To add new friends, tap the Friends tab to view your current friends list and then tap the '+' icon in the top-left corner. Then enter an email address or nickname (if you know it).

Your personal Game Center

Finding your way around your gaming hub

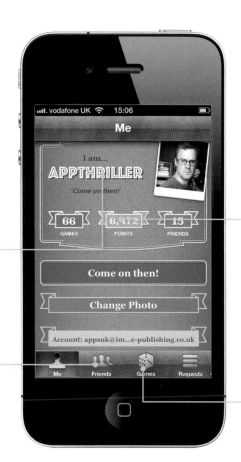

Your profile
Your nickname, status and photo will be proudly displayed on the main 'Me' page of your Center app. Tap the photo and text box to change them

Game Center Sections
You can easily jump to your friends list, the games currently on your device (and thousands that aren't) and find friends via the tabs at the bottom of the screen

Your Game Center score
Achievements you earn in compatible games are calculated into scores which are added to your running total. This is your overall Game Center score to compare with your friends'

Online gaming
All of your iPhone gaming is channelled through Game Center, including the ability to play against your friends online. Ensure that both you and your friend have the same game installed on your device and then select the multiplayer options. You can now connect through Game Center and give them a sound thrashing.

Recommended games
Tap on the Games tab to view lists of compatible games. Tap on an icon to be taken to the App Store to learn more about the game and purchase it

4: Get games
Tap on the Games tab and you can view all the compatible games on your device. You can get more games by tapping the 'Game Recommendations' at the top of the page.

5: Earn achievements
You earn achievements and points by completing feats within games. To view a game's available achievements, tap Games and then choose a game and tap Achievements.

6: Friend recommendations
New to iOS 5 is a feature that recommends new friends based on the games you play and existing friends. In the Friends tab, tap Recommendations in the top-left corner.

Essential apps

Must-have downloads for your iPhone

"Apps that will enhance your life and provide hours of fun"

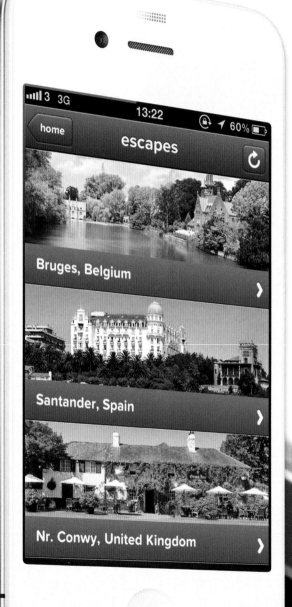

The Essential iPhone Apps

The must-have apps to enhance your iPhone's functionality

Apps are easily one of the biggest selling points of the iPhone. The number available is staggering, with new ideas and creations being uploaded every day. And the sheer simplicity of purchasing and immediacy has meant they have sold by the millions, with something for everyone. So whether you want to while away a few hours on a long journey, help keep your life in order or get more work done away from the office, there are an array of top apps that will extend the functionality of your iPhone no end.

Productivity

The iPhone comes with a healthy selection of productivity features which are designed to cover the basics, but there are apps available that can extend the core functionality and in many cases offer the ability to do things that you would have previously not thought possible on a phone. From Cloud-based storage services to advanced word processors, there are countless apps available in every productivity area that will help you get through a busy day, and also many apps designed to target specific industries or job types. Productivity can cover a wide range of uses, but here we will show you some of the best solutions available for the device and some that will make your iPhone use much more productive than before. You may even find that you can use an iPhone in place of a laptop for many tasks, making it one of the most useful items in your life.

"You may find you can use an iPhone in place of a laptop for many tasks"

iStudiez Pro

Price: £1.99/$2.99   **Developer:** Enfiero Incorporated

 Schools and colleges are busy places and the schedules can be bewilderingly challenging. This app helps students organise the work they need to do before each class and, make sure they actually get to each lesson on time.

■ The design of the app brings the crucial data to the front with ease.

Dropbox

Price: Free
Developer: Dropbox, Inc

 Dropbox is well known for offering quick and simple access to as many files as you need online and the official app makes the service even more worthwhile. Indeed, the presentation is so cleverly put together that you may prefer using Dropbox with an iPhone rather than through a desktop computer.

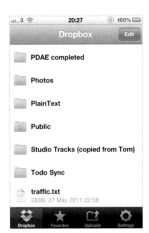

■ You could not ask for a simpler interface for this app.

Todo

Price: £2.99/$4.99
Developer: Appigo, Inc

There are literally hundreds of To Do managers in the App Store, but some stand out above the rest and Todo is a good example. It offers a crisp view of your current tasks and also enables the management of projects in a simplistic interface. Synchronisation is catered for by various methods and it is likely to be preferred by the majority who try it. For all types of task management, Todo is a great option.

■ Behind the simple exterior is a serious task management system.

Dolphin Browser

Price: Free
Developer: MotoTap Inc

 For many tasks outside of apps, the web browser is likely the first destination to find information, catch up on the news and do so much more. Dolphin Browser offers a speedy web experience with tab functionality, unique gesture control and a smart address bar to speed up access. It is a solution that builds on the Safari browser and one which makes every website feel more suited to the mobile form.

■ The gesture feature is unique and wonderful to use.

Numbers

Price: £6.99/$8.99
Developer: iTunes S.A.R.L.

 If your line of work requires creating, viewing and editing spreadsheets then Numbers is an intuitive app built around a lovely interface that allows you to construct spreadsheets from scratch or use pre-created templates. You are given full freedom to add tables, charts, photos and graphics, using your fingers to orchestrate the process. When putting together your sheets you can choose from over 250 easy-to-use functions, enter data and then use sliders, steppers and pop-ups to explore the results. Working on your iPhone has never been easier.

■ Creating lovely looking sheets is a breeze with Numbers.

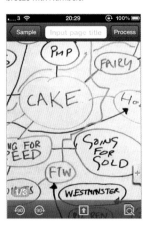

Awesome Note (+To-do/ Diary)

Price: £2.49/$3.99
Developer: BRID

 Not all note applications are the same and Awesome Note is proof of that. Besides an interface that is fully customisable and which looks professional in every way, it has excellent synchronisation features that make it the perfect companion to services like Evernote. Each note can include photos, locations and backgrounds which also makes it fun to build new tasks, receipts and general notes. It is close to being the perfect mobile notes app.

■ The main interface is beautiful to look at and use.

CamScanner+

Price: £2.99/$4.99 **Developer:** IntSig Information Co, Ltd

 Much of the world still revolves around paper and digitising these documents can make organisation much easier in the future. CamScanner+ is ideal for this task because it creates crisp reproductions of paper documents and helps you to organise them in a manner which perfectly suits the way you work.

■ Scans can be captured in great detail.

"There are countless productivity apps available to help you work efficiently"

Torch®

Price: Free
Developer: Intellectual Flame

 This app has been lurking high in the free charts in the App Store for years – and for good reason. Everyone needs a torch at one time or another, and this app utilises the flash of your iPhone's camera to simple, yet useful effect by making it act as a torch. It's surprisingly bright too, offering instant illumination whenever you need it. You can even use it as a strobe light – which is especially handy for parties or pop concerts! With so many apps cluttering up the store that are completely useless, this one could never be accused of being that.

■ This is pretty much it as far as the Torch interface goes.

Keynote

Price: £6.99/$9.99 **Developer:** Apple Inc

 Creating presentations is never easy, but Apple has managed to make the process enjoyable. Keynote is gesture driven and the way it works on the iPhone shows that anything is possible on a smartphone and is worthy of consideration for anyone who needs to create presentations.

■ Keynote looks surprisingly similar to many PC presentation apps.

Pages

Price: £6.99/$9.99 **Developer:** Apple Inc

 Pages is one of the most advanced word processors available for the iPhone and includes many features that are standard in the desktop version. Templates for letters, flyers and other tasks are included alongside the standard font and colour management. Where the app excels, however, is in the way touch is used to manipulate images and the text. It balances the need to cram in a myriad of features alongside the natural limitations of the smaller screen very well indeed and works exactly as you would like it to.

Lifestyle

The most wide-ranging app category of all is lifestyle and can encompass many different types of apps. From social networking to photography, the subjects are unlimited and can be more influential for your daily needs than you may expect. They often have a practical slant, such as helping you to create and manage blogs, and also offer the perfect mix between fun and practicality when getting things done. If an app does not specifically fall into another category, it is likely to end up in the lifestyle section and this means that many apps you require will be available there. No matter what your needs and how diverse they are, it is likely that solutions will have been produced. Here we will highlight some of the best including some that are quirky enough to prove that the subject matter of iPhone apps is truly unlimited.

HeyTell

Price: Free **Developer:** Voxilate

 We have social networks, voicemail, and instant messaging, and now we have HeyTell which attempts to merge all three into one system that takes a unique approach to communication. You hold down a button on the main screen and speak a message, and when completed it is sent to a contact who can listen to the message. They can then send one back and so it continues. It sounds incredibly simple and it is, but it works perfectly and brings more personality to the world of instant messaging than we have seen previously. It is a unique and clever service.

■ Hold down the big record button and speak your message. It's simple.

"No matter what your needs and how diverse they are, there will be an app for them"

Twitter

Price: Free
Developer: Twitter, Inc

 With so many iPhone Twitter clients available on the App Store, choosing the one that suits you best is very difficult. It therefore makes sense to look at the official client first, which offers almost every feature you will need; retweets, favourites, direct messages, multimedia sharing and everything else is wrapped up in an interface that is as close to the desktop version. The app is free and stable, even on older iPhones, making it a solution that any discerning Twitter user will be happy to use.

■ Tweets are displayed similarly to the main Twitter page.

Momento

Price: £1.99/$2.99
Developer: d3i Ltd

 Keeping a diary is a highly personal task and requires a personalised environment to work in. Momento offers this alongside the ability to automatically import social networking activity and photos to highlight what has happened each day. The interface has been created with great care and can cope with displaying your feeds from Twitter, YouTube and many other online services, and it all comes together to offer a near perfect mobile diary which you will come to treasure.

■ The calendar view speeds up navigation.

Amazon Mobile

Price: Free
Developer: AMZN Mobile LLC

Amazon is known around the world for offering an attractive and easy online shopping experience and the company has taken this knowledge and produced a solution for the iPhone that makes a mockery of the smaller screen size the user has to deal with. Everything from the checkout process to the way the products are displayed make it perfectly usable whenever you need to make a purchase, for that forgotten birthday for example, and it truly is an example for others to follow.

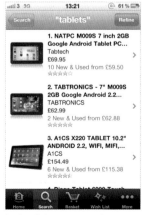

■ The whole Amazon catalogue is available through this app.

eBay

Price: Free
Developer: eBay Inc

 eBay can be tricky to use with the variety of products on offer and the number of different sellers. With different auction types and so many variables, this app does well to make the search process easy, whatever you are looking for. It takes some time to get used to, but the ability to use eBay 24 hours a day means you are much more likely to find a bargain.

■ Searching works just as well on the iPhone as on a desktop.

Groupon

Price: Free
Developer: Groupon, Inc

 The Groupon service provides members with ample opportunity to snap up great deals in their local area. These deals could include cheap hotel rooms, meals out, relaxing spa weekends or balloon flights, and this app will send you push notifications of the latest deals and allow you to view all available offers through an intuitive interface.

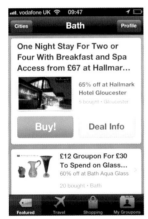
■ You can also gain inspiration for trips abroad.

Pizza Express

Price: Free
Developer: Pizza Express Restaurants

 If you like pizza and regularly visit Pizza Express restaurants then this is the perfect app as it allows you to find your nearest eaterie, browse the full menu, order takeaway or, best of all, settle your bill using your iPhone without having to wait around. It is perfect for when you're eating out with only a limited amount of time.

■ The interface is simple, but it works very efficiently.

The Photo Cookbook – Quick & Easy

Price: £2.99/$4.99 **Developer:** ditter. projektagentur GmbH

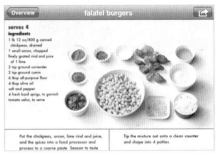 Cooking is about presentation as well as flavour and this is where an app like this one excels. It replicates the look and feel of a cookery book and combines expert instructions with some great photos to make the whole experience come alive.

■ The presentation of The Photo Cookbook is sublime.

Camera+

Price: £1.49/$1.99 **Developer:** Inventive, Inc

 Camera+ is seen by many as the ultimate iPhone camera app and the list of features suggests this to be a fair assessment. With stabilisation, exposure adjustments and many other features it can feel busy to use, but it is the perfect addition for any iPhone user who takes lots of photos.

■ Camera+ contains a wealth of features.

AroundMe

Price: Free **Developer:** Attorno A Me SRL

 There are many apps designed to offer information on the services available to you locally, but few are as quick as AroundMe. Choose a category and press the search button – that's all you need to do. A list including contact details and extra information will immediately pop up and you will wonder how you ever coped without it.

You can find any local establishment with AroundMe.

Entertainment

Entertainment apps encompass large swathes of practical applications from music to video and many other aspects that come together to make a smartphone more flexible and useful. There are hundreds of solutions that can fill in those times when you have a few minutes to spare. Everything from eBook reading to music management is covered and the gaming side has now reached a level which compares well with dedicated gaming consoles. You can create visual masterpieces, test your brain and listen to thousands of radio stations from a smartphone and do so much more under the guise of entertainment. Here we present the essential entertainment apps to get you started. The list is unlimited, but some apps stand out and are worthy considerations.

Kindle

Price: Free **Developer:** AMZN Mobile LLC

 There are many eBook readers available for the iPhone, but few rival the Kindle when it comes to the number of eBooks available. Besides being an excellently presented reader with a variety of presentation options, it will also synchronise your current reading position across an iPhone, iPad, PC and any other supported device so you can read how you want to whenever you like. It is hard to fault a solution that offers a huge library of competitively priced eBooks.

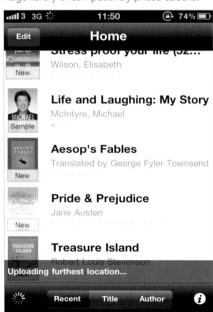

■ The number of Kindle eBooks available is huge.

Spotify

Price: Free
Developer: Spotify

 Many people see Spotify as the best alternative to iTunes and one which offers the perfect solution for those who are heavily into their music. Not only does this app offer the ability to stream songs to an iPhone, premium members also get the opportunity to listen to tracks offline. This means that you will have access to more than 13 million tracks whenever you like for a reasonable subscription charge.

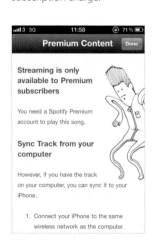

■ Premium members can also play tracks offline on an iPhone.

IMDb Movies and TV

Price: Free
Developer: IMDb

 IMDb is a big name in the world of movies and the official app is certainly not a disappointment. The amount of content that is accessible through this application is tremendously complete and includes everything from the latest movies through to award winners. This app will prove itself very useful for movie buffs and anyone else with an interest in television and movies.

■ The entire range of visual entertainment is covered.

Words With Friends

Price: £1.49/$1.99
Developer: Newtoy, Inc

 Few games bring people together as successfully as *Words With Friends* does. Think of it as a version of *Scrabble*, but one that lets you make moves which are then sent to your opponent over the internet. You will be alerted when they have made their move and so the game continues. It is an engrossing experience and one that can help develop friendships over long games spanning weeks or months.

■ The game board and pieces are very similar to *Scrabble*.

Angry Birds

Price: £0.69/$0.99
Developer: Rovio Mobile

If you haven't heard of *Angry Birds*, you have probably been living underground for the past year. It is a phenomenon that has expanded way beyond smartphones, but this is because it is fundamentally a hugely addictive game that will keep you coming back time and time again. The developer regularly releases updates with new levels included to make the low asking price even batter value and this makes it 'the' essential game to install on any iPhone. Once you start flinging birds at pigs, you will wonder how you got through each day previously without at least a few minutes playing *Angry Birds*.

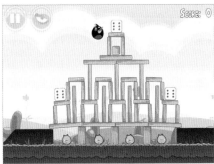

■ The premise of the game is simple, but it is highly addictive.

Brushes – iPhone Edition

Price: £2.99/$4.99   **Developer:** Steve Sprang

Brushes is a drawing app that blurs the lines between creativity and entertainment, but is without doubt a fun experience in the right hands. If you have the artistic talent you will get a great deal of satisfaction from the features and even those with lesser skills will enjoy the experience.

■ Anyone can create fabulous pictures.

Sky GO

Price: Free
Developer: BSkyB

The speed of modern day 3G and Wi-Fi connections means that video streaming apps like Sky GO can provide the level of experience we have been waiting for. Get access to channels you subscribe to with no extra charges. It brings the genuine Sky experience to the iPhone.

■ Sky GO is an example of video streaming done the right way.

Watch TV Free Live with TVCatchup

Price: Free
Developer: GZero Ltd

This app provides instant access to the popular website that allows registered users to watch a freeview channel live on their iPhone. As long as you have a Wi-Fi or 3G signal then you can enjoy a wealth of entertainment on the move.

■ You can technically carry a library of video on your iPhone with this app.

■ Thousands of radio stations are now at your fingertips.

BBC iPlayer

Price: Free
Developer: Media Applications Technologies Limited

This was the original TV catch-up vewing portal app released on the iPhone. It is still the best and has been emulated by all of its competitors. The app provides access to a rich wealth of BBC TV programmes that you can watch again whenever you want and it also features content from their extensive selection of radio stations. The service it provides is exceptional and the range of features impressive – a must for any iPhone user.

■ Carry the BBC around with you and watch a wealth of programmes.

"There are hundreds of apps available that can fill those spare gaps in your day with entertainment"

TuneIn Radio Pro

Price: £0.69/$0.99
Developer: Synsion Radio Technologiese SRL

Remember when a radio was a piece of plastic and a speaker that sat on the kitchen side? The iPhone can now be your radio and deliver more than 50,000 stations from around the world for a few pennies. This app delivers an experience that truly does make the world's radio stations mobile.

Price: £2.49/$3.99 **Developer:** Oceanhouse Media Inc

There's a Wocket in My Pocket!

Education and fun in one package

Children's books should be fun and colourful enough to grab the interest of the young, and should ideally take things further and offer some educational features such as the ability to learn new words. This interactive eBook does just that, cleverly blending the narration with highlights over each word, and even zooms words across the screen when the child taps each picture.

This is perfect for young children who are learning to read, and doesn't get in the way when older children are enjoying the experience and simply listening to the story. The sound effects raise the game further, and are individually tailored for each scene to bring the experience to life, and the narration is as professional as we have heard anywhere else. At the heart of any book, however, there has to be an exciting and engaging story. Thankfully, this particular tale is extremely amusing, and will let parents enjoy each page just as much as their children do.

The familiarity of the artwork is another positive, and the fact that it is taken directly from the original book helps a lot, with everything coming together well enough to create an authentic digital reproduction of a classic tale. Dr Seuss holds a special place in the hearts of many, and this book ensures that it is brought to the digital age without destroying any of the charm of the original. The silly rhymes and humorous phrases will stay in your head for a long time to come, and few books can produce the kind of reaction that this one does.

Perhaps the greatest positive is that it can be used by very young children to read alone and learn new words without the need for parents to be constantly standing over them. Of course, there is still an iPhone in their hands, so maybe some adult guidance wouldn't be such a bad thing just in case they get too excited by the whole experience, which – it has to be said – is rather impressive.

Rating ★★★★★

■ The personalities of the characters in the story shine through, making this enjoyable for adults as well as children

■ The simplicity of the graphics helps to tell the story in a fun and endearing manner

■ Tap a particular item, and its name will pop up on the screen in word form, thus aiding word-association skills

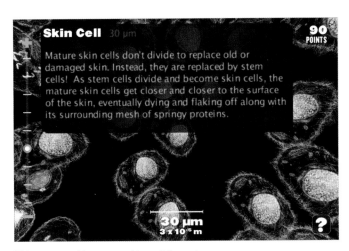

Skin Cell 30 μm

90 POINTS

Mature skin cells don't divide to replace old or damaged skin. Instead, they are replaced by stem cells! As stem cells divide and become skin cells, the mature skin cells get closer and closer to the surface of the skin, eventually dying and flaking off along with its surrounding mesh of springy proteins.

30 μm
3 × 10⁻⁵ m

■ Learn everything you could possibly want to know about the human hand

Price: £1.49/$1.99 Developer: Green-Eye Visualization

Powers of Minus Ten – Cells and Genetics

Explore the human hand and the basic biology behind it

Budding biologists will certainly enjoy exploring this app. Zoom in on a human hand, and take a scientific tour of the cells and genetics. Zoom in to the skin's surface, and then delve a little further to discover cells, cell parts, mitosis, DNA replication, translation and transcription.

Built just like a game, you are able to collect points when opting to interact with an area, although there are no rewards or quizzes included as you might expect from a game.

This interactive app is extremely easy to use, and well designed. Responding quickly to touch, you can zoom in and out with ease, or use the zoom bar to jump between layers.

It's not overly expensive, but you are limited to just touring the human hand. It is, however, a good start to what could become a great scientific series.

Rating ★★★★☆

Price: Free Developer: RBS

NatWest Stockbrokers App

Great for Brokerline account holders

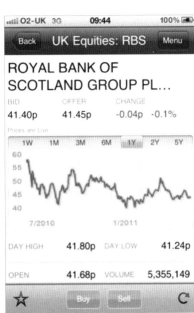

An app for customers to access Stockbrokers Brokerline accounts and trade on the move.
The ability to view orders, track portfolios and create a watch list, this app provides at-a-glance account summaries, up-to-the-minute trade prices, real-time quotes on stock you are monitoring and a detailed breakdown of your portfolio, current holdings, market value and overall gain or loss. It's also highly secure to use.

This app combines an attractive and accessible interface with a high level of detailed information that is relayed very effectively, even on the small screen. But there's still room for improvement. We would have liked the landscape orientation to have been utilised to allow users to interact with graphs to see the prices at specific points, and the option to transfer money in or out of your account is lacking. A promising start.

Rating ★★★★☆

■ The interface is well designed and easy to navigate, giving you info when you need it

■ Sadly, the option to transfer money in or out of your account is missing at present

■ Work out monthly costs easily

■ There are plenty of properties to view

Price: £2.99/$4.99 **Developer:** BBC Worldwide LTD

Kirstie and Phil's House Hunter

Get help searching for a new home from TV's experts

If you're in the process of or planning on moving soon, and are becoming a little overwhelmed, you might be interested in the BBC's app featuring Kirstie Allsopp and Phil Spencer, two TV hosts who know a fair bit about the housing market.

The app gives you everything you need when moving house. You can search for new properties, and calculate budgets and contact agents, all from within the app itself. It's also possible to set the criteria for your dream home, with the option to save, score and make notes on other properties that you view. You can take photos as you view properties, and save them to your database. If you're just looking for advice, there are plenty of written tips, as well as video and audio advice from the two TV stars.

It may cost more than some apps, but with so much information at your fingertips, it's hard to fault Kirstie and Phil's House Hunter if you're looking for a new home.

Rating ★★★★☆

Price: £2.49/$3.99 **Developer:** Med ART Studios LLC

Pregnancy

Personalise your pregnancy!

Pregnancy is an exciting time, and certainly one of the most important events in the life of a family. This app is very much a kind of pregnancy calendar. It's easy to use, and the most notable feature is the ability to be able to view your baby's development week-by-week courtesy of some stunning foetal images. Tap the 'My Baby' option, and you'll see exactly what we mean – the graphics really are first class. Tap a circle that appears on the foetal image, and you'll see comments that explain just how the developmental process is unfolding. For example, did you know that the vocal chords are already developing by week 13? Other features include an organiser function that logs your antenatal appointments and a to-do list that lets you manage pregnancy-related tasks. Also included are a kick timer and a useful contraction timer. You can even use the app to share your baby's developmental progress with friends and family via Facebook.

Rating ★★★★★

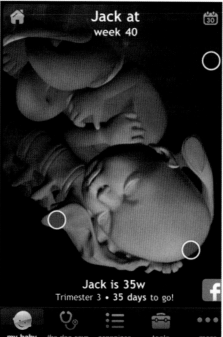

■ Follow your baby's developmental progress based on the actual due date

■ An interactive Pregnancy Timeline adjusts to your baby's weekly milestones

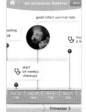

Price: Free Developer: Working Transitions

Infinity CV Builder

Create a CV while on the go

Creating a good CV can be a difficult first hurdle for any jobseeker, and not fully knowing what information to include and how to structure it can be a stressful situation. Infinity CV Builder is a free iPhone-sized CV creation tool and job advice wizard.

Creating a CV is a simple process where the user is prompted for the relevant information for each section, and the app offers advice on what kinds of details to include. Each section also includes audio clips that offer advice on how to deliver a CV with impact. Once the CV is finished, it can be previewed within the app and then printed, tweeted or emailed directly to a potential employer.

The additional 'Job Tips' section includes a generous 50 tips spread over five topics. It's an excellent resource. For any jobseeker looking for help, Infinity CV Builder is a superb free app.

Rating ★★★★★

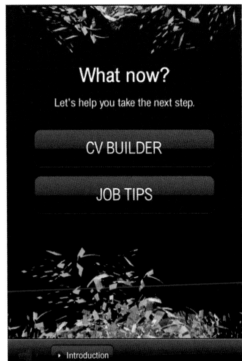

■ The app consists of two sections: CV Building and Job Tips

Price: Free Developer: FDV Solutions

UN Foundation

Stay informed to get involved

The UN Foundation app enables you to stay up to date with global events as they unfold. Likely to appeal to users who are interested in current affairs, charity work and aid efforts, this informative app keeps you on track with developments around the world.

You can browse, search and check out all of the latest charity campaigns, and share stories, photos and videos with others via social networking sites such as Facebook and Twitter. There is even a 'Give' feature that enables you to select a cause and donate on the go. Use the app to check out all the latest issues that the UN Foundation is committed to working on and improving, including climate change, poverty, children's health, peace and security. You can even sign up for email alerts.

UN Foundation is worth the download time, giving you the chance to stay informed and make a difference.

■ Donate directly to a cause through the 'Give' icon via text or credit card

■ Read current news stories on the home screen as soon as the app loads

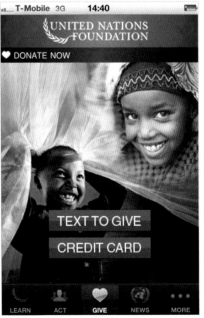

Rating ★★★★★

Price: £0.69/$0.99 Developer: Artem Demidenko

Numberama

Take on the old puzzle game

Number-based games have really taken off in the last few years, and if you enjoy puzzles like Sudoku you'll almost certainly love Numberama. Based on a game played in the Eighties and Nineties, the premise is easy enough to understand, but the game itself is surprisingly difficult.

You are able to 'cross out' two of the same numbers when they are next to each other, or if the two numbers have a sum of ten. You can cross out similar numbers or two numbers that add up to ten, even if there are empty squares between them, just as long as they are aligned, and you are also able to pass across lines as if you were reading a book to remove numbers. Once all the possible pairings have been made, you can tap a button, and all the remaining numbers are re-written below in the same order, only without the gaps. The aim is to remove all the numbers from the board.

While this sounds simple enough in theory, it's actually much harder than it first appears, giving you a real challenge on your first attempt. In fact, the game soon became a really compulsion, and we found ourselves having "just one more go" on several occasions. Much like Sudoku, the game is incredibly addictive, and hugely rewarding when you successfully complete it.

The app has two modes – a Classic mode with numbers 1-19, and a Random mode that scrambles them. There is an undo button in the bottom left, so if you regret an earlier decision you can go back, and a full-screen button in the lower right. Along the bottom are the options to view your high scores, read the rules or share your game with others. Upon opening the app, there were no obvious rules, which was rather confusing, so we'd like to see them included as an opening screen. Aside from this, the app did everything we asked of it, and was a lot of fun. The puzzles are really tough to finish, but really rewarding when you do as a result. Puzzle aficionados will love it, and for such a low price it won't break the bank either.

Rating ★★★★★

■ Apparently the Random game is more difficult, although we found it more fun just because it was always different

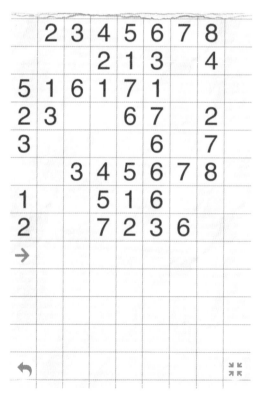

■ You can play in full-screen, which allows for more numbers

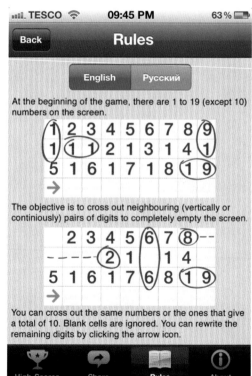

■ The in-app icons are easy to understand, and allow you to create sequences and have fun with the music

Price: Free Developer: Moderati, Inc

Romplr: Remix

Remix songs and see if you can make the charts

 Making mixing a competitive business, Romplr: Remix is a combination of music app and game in which you have to remix tracks in order to earn points and make the charts for that song.

You have the option to download some genuine chart-toppers from the in-app store, or use the free mixkits to put together your own beats. You earn points for everything you put together coherently, with a lot of the high-level technical issues such as beat timing done automatically so that you can focus on creating combos and sequences.

Additionally, the in-game dashboard is very simple to operate, with various icons representing the different musical tools that you can mix into the track within your 90-second time limit. You can then compare your score to others in the chart and see where you rank. You can enter freestyle mode and simply hone your skills if you would prefer.

The setbacks are the long loading time on each track, and the prices of in-app purchases for any tracks by major artists.

Despite the minor snags, if you've got the patience to sit through the long loading screen, you'll probably find Romplr to be a worthwhile download, particularly if you love your music, as this app makes for a very interactive experience.

Rating ★★★★☆

Price: Free Developer: Autodesk

Pixlr-o-matic

Make your photos stand out with Pixlr-o-matic

 While there are plenty of apps available that allow you to make subtle effect changes to your photographs, Pixlr-o-matic looks to have trumped them all with its sheer range of effects that have the ability to make your random snapshots look like vintage – and on occasions – professional photography.

Firstly, the app looks great, giving you the impression you're in your very own dark room, and the interface is smooth and quick, even when you're in the process of applying effects. The photos appear in an instant, giving you the chance to swipe through them effortlessly until you find something that catches your eye. Moreover, the process of enhancing your image also turns out to be reasonably straightforward.

It's also refreshing that Pixlr-o-matic deals with your photos first, giving you the choice of taking a photo or uploading one, rather than simply asking you to settle on your effect before choosing your image. This allows for a more enjoyable experience, as you can spend ages scrolling through effects and lighting changes as you see fit in order to observe exactly how each one alters the photo.

Of course, given all the choice that is available here, it can sometimes be hard to settle on an effect, which is why it's great that you have the option of coming back later and editing your photos, rather than having to decide and share straight away.

 There are great saving options on display, with the ability to upload to Flickr, Facebook and Dropbox. It's this area where the iOS version of the app trumps the Android version as these options currently aren't available anywhere except on the iPhone.

Rating ★★★★★

■ Brilliant retro effects and the lack of a price make this one to add to the 'essentials' list

Price: £0.69/$0.99 Developer: Com2us USA, Inc.

Inotia 3: Children of Carnia
Earn your +7 to screen-tapping ability

RPGs are renowned for their wealth of content. Whether it's the hours of storylines, levelling up or combat system, there are very few RPGs that do not at least offer a decent amount of options. As the genre moves to smartphones, it's games like Inotia 3: Children of Carnia that pave the way for how the genre can work well on these smaller devices.

The sheer amount of options here is outstanding, especially considering that the app is completely free. While the story is typical of RPGs, it's intriguing enough to draw you in, and never interfered with long enough to become boring – you don't want

to be sat reading text instead of playing while on the train or bus, and thankfully you will not have to here.

Combat is played in real time, with a standard attack and any of the chosen hotkey buttons. Unlike many RPGs you find on smartphones, auto aim is included to assist in any awkward positioning, which is useful. Activated abilities give you control over how your damage is dealt, while AI party members do an extremely good job of making themselves relevant without taking all of the good kills.

It's not all smooth sailing, though, it has to be said. While the hotkey bar is entirely customisable, the 'Shop' button close to your first ability is a little too nearby and therefore liable to being accidentally tapped.

That's not the only downside, as there are the advertisements that appear between each map. We're not so naïve as to expect that a free app shouldn't need funding somehow, but this is one of the worst examples of in-game ads that we have seen yet. Then there's the quest system, which falls back on fetch quests to prolong things too often.

Despite all this, Inotia has enough depth to sustain many hours of play, providing you can forgive its flaws. We found that its entertainment value outweighed its flaws, and were generally very happy with it.

Rating ★★★★☆

■ As the game progresses, Inotia's difficulty level quickly rises

■ The world you explore is huge and varied. I's a shame the quests let it down

■ The storyline is typical, but good for those looking for an enjoyable tale

GoToMyPC

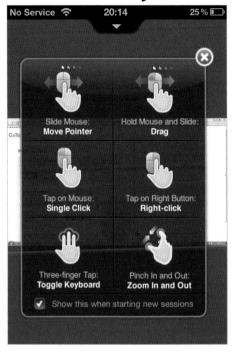

■ Once connected, the pop-up display will outline the main controls

■ The installation process is easy to follow

Price: Free   Developer: Citrix

Remote control computer trickery

GoToMyPC is a remote control software service that enables a user to operate their computer from another device over the internet. In recent times the service has branched out to iOS, allowing control from an iPhone or iPad.

An active subscription is required to use the service, although free trials are available that last for 30 days with no up-front requirement for payment information. Considering the complicated technical aspects involved in network connections such as this, the installation process of GoToMyPC is reassuringly easy. Once the client is installed on a computer, simply enter the same account details on the app and the two will connect. Upon startup, the app displays the various ways of controlling the computer via a touch device, easing new users into the app in the process.

The response time works well and the initially strange controls become more intuitive over time. As an easy-to-install remote computer solution, GoToMyPC is hard to beat.

Rating ★★★★★

Viz Profanisaurus
Das Krapital   Euphemisms and dirty definitions

Price: £1.49/$1.99   Developer: Dennis Publishing

■ See which profanities other users rate as the best, using the Favourites tab

Not for the easily offended, but if you're open to a little blue humour then you're in for a treat and will always have the perfect euphemism for the occasion. Not only does it contain a full dictionary of profanities, but there is also the link icon, which brings up the definitions of any additional slang mentioned, so you're never lost in the joke. The random generator greets you upon opening the app with a phrase from the dictionary. One swipe, and you can spice up your Facebook and Twitter posts with the uploader that creates a filthy sentence for you. One more swipe takes your phrase and creates a spider diagram of terms you might enjoy. You can also use the search tool.

This is a well designed app, and the developers have obviously listened to consumers, because the Profanisaurus is no longer a sometimes unintelligible jumble of euphemisms; now, it's a clear and concise dirty dictionary.

■ Definitions come with a link option to explain any other euphemisms in the text

Rating ★★★★☆

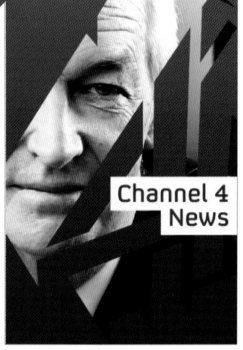

■ There are sections dedicated to blogs from the channel's journalists

Price: Free Developer: Channel 4

C4 News

Channel 4 becomes the latest station to join the dedicated news app

In its traditional purple, the Channel 4 News app is a good addition to the home screen of anyone who likes to stay on top of the news.

The app doesn't overload on multimedia clips, with just two pages of main headlines, which you can swipe between. The bottom tab bar allows you to search for the news the way you want to, be it by headline or category. There are sections dedicated to blogs from the channel's journalists, with a short archive of all their recent posts. In addition, there is a special reports tab, made up of a collection of articles grouped together to form part of a key subject in the news.

A dedicated gallery section contains a 'pictures of the week' gallery, as well as archives on big news stories. So while the multimedia content isn't as in-your-face as some other news apps, it does exist if you look for it.

Arguably the best feature is the presence of a catch-up tab, which allows you to view all the Channel 4 news bulletins from the last seven days, just in case you missed one and wanted to get back on top of the issues.

Rating ★★★★☆

Opuss

Price: Free Developer: Seamonster Ltd

A tweeting app that lets you write as much as you want

This app is a neat way to digest people's thoughts and feelings and post your own comments without being restricted to the 140 characters that Twitter imposes. Simply create your own account and can then go about reading other people's posts and following them, and can write, post and share your own comments within the growing community. The interface is very sophisticated and slick, and finding content to read is never a problem thanks to a 'Find' feature that breaks down posted content into 'Joke', 'Poem', 'Quote' and so on. Scouring the posts of other users indicates that the user base is a sensitive lot who weave words majestically in poems about self-harming and isolation, which is balanced with original and witty jokes. It champions good writing, so if you are in need of inspiration or uplifting prose then it's a great download that deserves to grow into something epic.

Rating ★★★★☆

■ Content can be easily filtered to find what you want

■ You can follow the posts of other users exactly as you would in Twitter

■ Once created, you can share your kinos via Facebook or Twitter

■ The secret is to select the part of the image that contains the movement

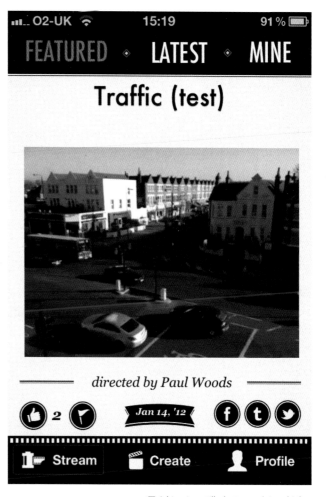

■ A kino is a still photograph in which a minor and repeated movement occurs

Price: Free **Developer:** Radu Spineanu

Kinotopic

Be creative and add cinemagraphs to images

Cinemagraphs are still photographs in which a minor and repeated movement occurs. A good example is a landscape panorama with flowers gently moving in the wind in the foreground. Cinemagraphs can give the illusion that you are actually watching a video, and are often created by taking a series of photographs or a video recording and, using image-editing software, compositing the photographs or video frames into a loop of sequential frames using the industry GIF file format in such a manner that motion in part of the subject between exposures is perceived as a repeating motion. This is in contrast to the stillness of the rest of the image.

Kinotopic is a fantastic app, and one that lets you create cinemagraphs – or kinos, as the developer calls them – on your iPhone. The app is relatively easy to use, and once you've created some images, you can impress others by using the tools provided to post them to Facebook, Twitter or Tumblr.

First, however, you will need to set up an account before you can create your first kino. Enter your details, tap 'Sign Up', and you're ready to go. So how does the app work? The first step is to create a three-second video clip that contains the movement you're interested in. Select an anchor frame, and the app will automatically remove camera-shake. Now, use a finger to select the part of the clip that contains the movement. Tap 'Create Kino', and your kino will be uploaded and available for you to preview. Mark it as private if you don't want it to be published in the developer's stream and available for other users to view.

All in all, Kinotopic is an innovative app that achieves exactly what it sets out to do without making the process too complex. Although it will take a little bit of practice to hone your kino-creating skills, the finished results are sure to impress your friends and family!

Rating ★★★★★

■ You can view a weather forecast for just about anywhere in the world

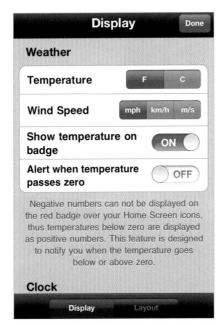

Display   Done

Weather

Temperature   F   C

Wind Speed   mph   km/h   m/s

Show temperature on badge   ON

Alert when temperature passes zero   OFF

Negative numbers can not be displayed on the red badge over your Home Screen icons, thus temperatures below zero are displayed as positive numbers. This feature is designed to notify you when the temperature goes below or above zero.

Clock

Display   Layout

■ Imperial and metric units are supported

▾ **Stoke Edith,** Surrey

50 °F   **Partly Cloudy**

Feels like **49**°   High **49**° Low **42**°

04 45 PM **27** December Tuesday

Humidity **71** %   Precipitation **0** inches   7 mph   Pressure **30.42** inches   Visibility **6.2** miles

| 6:00 PM 47° | 9:00 PM 45° | 12:00 AM 41° | 3:00 AM 45° | 6:00 AM 45° | 9:00 AM 42° | 12:00 PM 44° | 3:00 PM 44° |

WED 45° 38°   THU 45° 35°   FRI 49° 42°   SAT 53° 47°

■ The interface sports a wealth of weather forecasting data

Price: £0.69/$0.99   Developer: MYW Productions

Weather Live
Instant access to local weather conditions and forecasts

There are myriad weather forecasting tools available for the iPhone, but if you are a frequent traveller or outdoor enthusiast who relies on accurate weather forecasts, then Weather Live may well prove to be the app for you. Designed primarily as a service that provides live local weather updates, the app gives iPhone users instant access to a massive network of weather stations situated around the world. The interface is stunning, and whether it's sunny, raining or snowing, the app features polished animations that reflect current weather conditions wherever you happen to be. As a bonus, the animations are dynamic, and rather cleverly they change to suit the current weather conditions.

The screen is literally awash with weather information. For example, as well as being able to choose to display the local time for the selected city or location, you get instant access to the current temperature (including a 'feels like' temperature), wind speed and direction, humidity, pressure and even visibility. The

bottom of the display shows you the general weather conditions for the next seven days, as well as three-hourly reports.

Some handy personalisation options are included, one of the most notable of which is support for adding multiple locations. Changing location is a breeze – just swipe a finger across the screen. You can also opt to display wind speed and temperature using imperial or metric units, with the current temperature being displayed as an icon badge on your home screen. You can even receive alert notifications when the temperature falls below zero, and adjust the screen brightness by swiping a finger vertically.

In fact, the only slight niggle we found was that the app initially failed to automatically find our location accurately. However, this isn't a problem, as it's easy to add a location manually. All in all, it's a first-class weather forecasting tool, and one that offers the roving iPhone user exceptionally good value for money.

Rating

Price: Free Developer: XLabz Technologies Pvt. Ltd.

GeoSocials–Play. Win. Socialize.

Play games and hunt treasure with those around you

Every so often, we get stuck at a train station and find ourselves looking for ways to pass the time. GeoSocials is a new way to do that, but at the same time interact with those around us who could be in the same position.

The app uses a combination of GPS social networking and a selection of mini-games to allow you to socialise at the same time as taking on challenges set by other players. This leads to the Treasure Hunt section, where you seek out diamonds on the map, each representing potential points should you complete the set challenge. All of these diamonds are user-generated, and you can place them yourself. The bigger the community gets, the more points you can get hold of. Real life rewards and discounts can also follow.

This adds a nice competitive nature, with leaderboards for local and global scores. It's from the leaderboards that you can seek out players, view full profiles and add them as friends.

Rating ★★★★★

■ Use the map to seek out treasure near you

■ Use the dashboard to navigate

■ Heading into the app's settings allows you to change match details

■ Scoring in Court Buddy is as simple as tapping on your iPhone's screen

Price: Free Developer: Dark Peak Digital Limited

Court Buddy

Keep track of squash scores

Designed to replicate traditional paper scoring cards, Court Buddy allows you to track squash and UK racketball on your iPhone using an extremely simple tap-to-score interface. The scoreboard loads instantly with the app, meaning you're never going to get caught out by a game that starts prematurely. Whenever a player scores, simply tap on their scoreboard.

Inside the app's settings, you can change details like player name, club and handicap, as well as the match venue name to ensure that you've got a solid record of every game. You can even export these from the main menu via email, or tweet a score if you want to broadcast it to the rest of the world.

Court Buddy is a simple app that serves its purpose well. There's no learning curve with it and, although basic, it certainly includes just about every feature you would require in this situation. The only improvement would be an option to remove the ads.

Rating ★★★★★

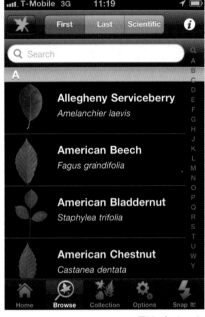

■ Preview other images that relate to the leaf

■ Search through the database of species in alphabetical order

■ Via the icon in the top-left corner you can search a range of species

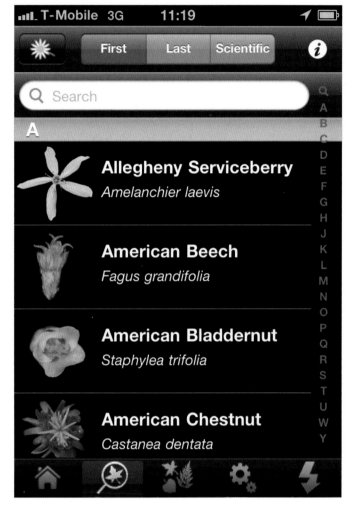

Price: Free   Developer: Peter Belhumeur

Leafsnap

Trees of northeast America

Curious minds and green-fingered enthusiasts will find Leafsnap a great app tool when they are out and about exploring greenery that is native to the northeast of America.

This fantastic app currently has 184 species in its database with over 2,590 high-resolution, illustrative images to browse through. Still in its early stages, this resource has a lot of promise and will continue to be developed.

Easy to use, the app has been well designed with enough layers and features to keep anyone engaged. Select the Browse option from the bottom menu to search through the database by leaf, flower, seed or berry. Once you've selected the correct species, you are able to preview other images that relate to the leaf and find out more information about the particular tree from which it originates.

The fantastic interactive Snap It! feature is what really makes this app stand out, enabling you to photograph a leaf before

presenting possible match results. You can browse through alternative tree types from which your leaf may have originated, selecting the most suitable one to label. Your leaf will then appear as part of your own collection database, which you can continue to build upon. A great way to encourage regular use, the Snap It! feature will only work when your iOS device is connected to the internet via Wi-Fi or 3G, which unfortunately is not practical if you are out exploring in the wilderness. It is worth noting, however, that you can still take a photograph in the app without internet connection to match up with results later on when you have found a Wi-Fi area, which is something.

Overall this is a very well thought-out app with the potential to be great – it just needs a little more development to make it a fantastic pocket companion. Because it is free, though, it's well worth the download to check out the database, and perhaps we will see further developments in the future.

Rating

■ The physics of collisions really are quite realistic

■ Showboating nets you more points

Price: £0.69/$0.99 **Developer:** NaturalMotion Games Limited

Icebreaker Hockey™

Still breaking backs, now on ice

A spin-off from the Backbreaker series, the premise is simple: get your player from one end of the rink to the other, and score. Unfortunately, there are a number of angry men from the opposing team in your way, requiring players to jink, twist, sprint and outmanoeuvre their opponents. It's a score attack game, meaning that the higher your points, the better you've done, so you'll be wanting to hit as many score zones and do as much showboating as possible to push that number through the roof. Just try not to get walloped by the opposition, as the Euphoria physics engine makes those collisions look all too real, and all too painful.

Controls are simple – tilt to turn, tap on-screen buttons to dodge, sprint, showboat and shoot. It's responsive and easy to get used to, but there's rarely time to rest on your laurels. It's for that very reason that Icebreaker can be almost painfully addictive. The power of 'just one more go' is very strong in this one.

Rating ★★★★★

Price: Free **Developer:** Voxilate

HeyTell

Communicate for free with this voice message app

It must be somewhat disheartening when you've got a good idea for an app and then you see the project through to near completion, only to discover that all of the best names have been taken. HeyTell is a surprisingly decent means to send and receive free voice messages between users, but the name makes it sound like a naff battle cry from Street Fighter II. The interface is nice and simple; you just select other HeyTell users from your contacts list (if they don't have the app currently installed then you can send them a message inviting them to become a user) and then hold down a button to record and send whatever audio dialogue you want. Push Notifications are used to convey the arrival of new messages and the sound quality and standard of service is good. What's more, this app also works well as a walkie talkie and intercom, and the integrated geo location feature makes it handy for finding lost friends and guiding them to your destination.

Rating ★★★★★

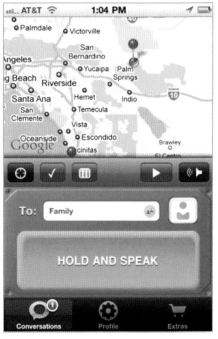

■ There are a host of additional features that you are able to add as in-app purchases

■ An integrated geo location feature lets you track your friends on a map

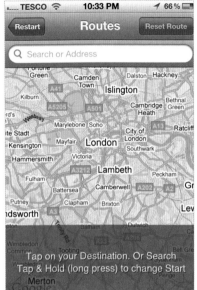

■ You will be given every route between locations

■ Simply tap on your chosen destination

Price: £1.99/$2.99 Developer: Azdev Ltd

BusMapper Pro

Live Routing and Bus Stops

If you decide to use the London bus system, this app might be very useful. It will use location data to find where you, and you can select a final destination. You can also select two separate areas and find the best route between them. When the app has found the two locations, you will be presented with every possible bus route and number represented. You can tap through the bus numbers to view your choices, and if the two places are close enough, the app will even tell you that you would be able to make the journey with a short walk instead.

The interface is clear, and the idea behind the app is so simple that it's always obvious what you need to do. Tapping a location on the map will select it as your destination, and you can also set a Home location, which will then be saved. It's a great little tool and one we'd like to see venture a little further than just London. Fingers crossed for the future.

> "You'll be presented with every possible bus route and number"

Rating ★★★★☆

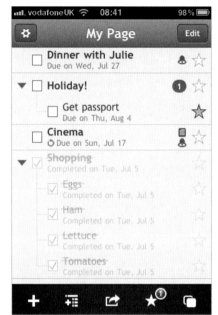

■ Each task can be given a reminder time, as well as other additional details

■ You can assign stars to specific tasks so that they stand out from others

Price: £1.99/$2.99 Developer: Hand Carved Code, LLC

Priorities

Is this 'to-do' app worth adding to your list?

There are no amazing standout features here that you won't find elsewhere, but there's also nothing important missing from this app either.

The core component of Priorities is that the tasks you need to do can be allocated to different pages. You can have one for shopping, home, work and so on. This makes it quick and easy to find the task you're looking for, and provides a simple interface to keep up to date with your calendar. Each task can also be given sub-tasks, and with the option of setting individual reminders for everything, you'll have no excuse when you miss that important meeting.

One neat feature is that these pages can be shared with other users of Priorities, which is especially useful for, say, passing the shopping list onto another family member, or sending an itinerary to colleagues. Another welcome addition is the ability to sync your lists to your other iOS devices, but like most of the other features, this isn't unique to this app.

Rating ★★★★☆

Price: £3.99/$5.99   Developer: 3D4Medical.com

Skeletal System Pro II – (NOVA Series) – iPhone edition

Tap into the power of this anatomical learning tool

If this app looks familiar, it's because it has been used in a TV ad to demonstrate the functionality of the iPad. To give you an overview, this cutting-edge app sports a photo-realistic 3D model of the human skeleton that can be browsed, rotated and magnified. The app's primary use is as a learning tool for anyone studying human anatomy, but it can also be used as a reference guide courtesy of the index function, which allows you to select a single structure. Do this, and the app will automatically zoom in and identify it. The app will also appeal to educators in the field of healthcare, as not only can you visually show detailed bone structures to students or patients, but then use the images to help explain medical conditions or injuries.

The app is easy to navigate, and if you want to identify any region, bone, skeletal area or ligament, then simply tap the area, and the app will zoom in and provide a close-up view. You can also rotate bones, ligaments or skeletal areas, or 'slice' areas (where applicable) for a coronal, sagittal or transverse cut view. There's even a 'scalpel' button that lets you add or remove up to four layers of connective tissue. We particularly like the Quick Navigation feature; tap the icon on the toolbar at the bottom of the screen, and you can choose from a range of viewing options. Zoom in on a skeletal structure, tap the pin icon on the right-hand toolbar, and pins will help you identify key areas, which are clearly labelled in English and Latin.

The developers have been working in collaboration with Stanford University School of Medicine on an upgrade to the app for the best part of a year. At the time of writing, the iPhone version is due to be upgraded to Skeleton System Pro III very soon.

Rating ★★★★★

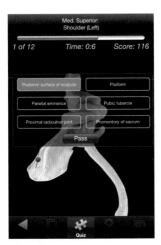

■ Use the quiz to test your anatomical knowledge

■ The Quick Navigation function lets you select an appropriate view

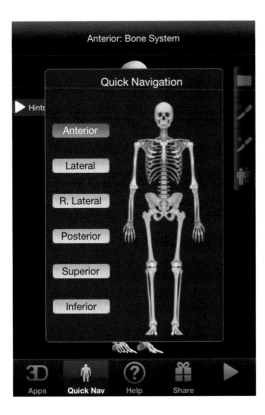

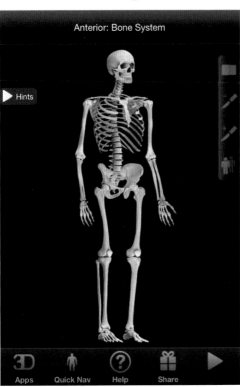

■ Utilising Location Services could make this app better

■ Being able to compare cars alongside each other is a useful feature

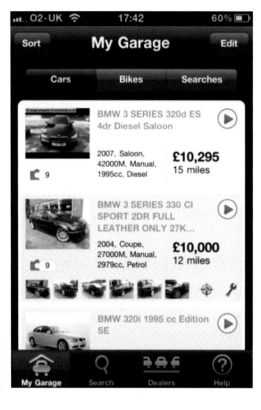

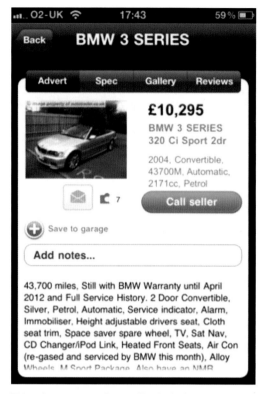

■ Simply tap on a car that you like the look of, in order to view the full ad

Price: Free **Developer:** Auto Trader

Auto Trader Mobile

Steer your way to your next car with this turbocharged app

The magazine and website are popular, but your iPhone makes car searching even easier.

The wide range of search customisation is impressive. First up is a postcode entry – oddly, the app doesn't make use of Location Services so you have to tell it where in the UK you are. It's one of the few areas where this app drops the ball. Next, state how far you want to travel for a new car .

Now the important bit – make and model. Select the former first, then you're presented with a list of models.

The next search criteria are particularly useful – minimum and maximum price. This can be tweaked later via a bar at the base of the screen. You can also specify colour, age, mileage, fuel, body type, number of doors, engine size and even seller type. And if all that isn't enough, there's also a free text entry box for keywords. It's extremely comprehensive, and very intuitive and easy to use.

We particularly like that if a car takes your fancy, you can tap on it and a new window appears with the full advert. There's a large window with photos of the car and all the important information

there for you at a glance. Importantly you also get the seller's details, plus you can visit the dealer's website (also within the app, which is excellent), share the ad and view a map showing the car's location. You can also email the seller for more information.

One of the best features of this app is the last button on the advert's screen: 'Save to garage'. This allows you to keep a selection of cars you're interested in. Enter the garage, and your dream motors are lined up for you to consider. Tap one and its full ad appears on the right. Now the clever bit – select up to three more cars from the garage and they all appear in a grid so you can compare them. These are the manufacturers' figures, however, and may not apply to the actual car being sold. Also, we found that for some cars, much of this data hasn't been entered, but this is equally a problem for Auto Trader's other outlets.

The Auto Trader app is well thought out, works speedily and is a joy to use. Now, where are the keys to our new Lamborghini?

Rating

Price: Free   Developer: Imagine Publishing

GamesTM

Games knowledge in your pocket

GamesTM has become one of the definitive UK gaming magazines; not just for its original audience of those who regularly buy console games, but also those at the other side of things – the games industry itself. The magazine even includes a recruitment section.

The iPhone version features all the content of the print publication, which ranges from reviews and in-depth insights into popular gaming franchises, such as Metal Gear, to a retro section, which in one recent issue focused on legendary football developers Sensible Software.

While there isn't much genuine interactivity in the iPhone version of the magazine, it's easy to navigate and simple to buy the issue you're after. Individual copies of the magazine (going back a couple of years to issue 84) can be bought instantly for £2.99 ($4.99) each – a discount on the cover price of the print version – but you can also download special collections for around a fiver, or grab an annual or six-month subscription.

Rating ★★★★☆

■ GamesTM is a great-looking magazine for console lovers

Price: £1.49/$1.99   Developer: return7

DebtMinder

Use your iPhone to clear debts

Getting into debt is never a pleasant experience, and without essential planning it's possible to let the problem get out of control. DebtMinder is an app that can analyse a user's financial situation, develop a payoff plan, and help dig them out of a hole.

DebtMinder offers simple and effective data synchronisation between iOS devices via the cloud, perfect for keeping team members updated on the current situation. Data can also be synced with sister app BillMinder. Syncing data is reliant upon setting up an account, but if you don't want to do this it is not required, as the app still works fine as a standalone product. DebtMinder calculates payoff plans based on interest rates, starting dates and opening. The progress of a plan can be viewed in the Reports section of the app where line graphs and pie charts visualise your current financial status. For someone looking to wrestle some control over their vanishing finances, DebtMinder is an ideal app for turning the tide.

Rating ★★★★☆

■ DebtMinder provides visual charts to track finances

Price: £0.69/$0.99   Developer: Streetline Media Pty Ltd

Campout

Discover new music in comfort

Campout is pitched as being like a music festival in your pocket, and while it has no real-life interactions or any kind of visual flair, you do get the opportunity to discover a wealth of new music without the discomfort of sitting in a muddy field with thousands of other people. The principle is simple: Campout plays you music from a pool of the Bandcamp website's independent artists, allowing you to discover new talent and listen to their artistic masterpieces. There's not much else to it, but it's a concept that we can really get on board with.

You have the option to click on 'Play Me Anything', in which the app will randomly select an artist for you, or you can search for a band if you know who you're looking for. There's also a Trending section where popular artists are showcased, and you can set albums as favourites in order to come back to them again. Additionally, you can click to view the artist in Bandcamp (out of the app), and there are thumbnails of the album artwork, but that's pretty much all this app features.

Campout is smooth to navigate, with four buttons at the bottom of the screen, and the design – which looks like an amp – is a nice touch. The songs are streamed, so it's best to use this app on a Wi-Fi connection, or else it will suck away at your data plan. The streaming takes seconds, though, and we experienced no long waiting times or tracks stopping for buffering.

Based on our experience, the songs in this app are generally an eclectic mix and of a high quality, so the chances are that your Favourites section will soon start to fill up. It may be lacking in fancy features or extra content, but what's here is very solid.

There are plenty of free radio-style apps out there that offer pretty much the same thing, but with over 100,000 artists in this collection, and a mere few coins to pay for it, there's not much to quibble about here. Campout is a nice addition to your music collection that could see you discovering your next new favourite band in no time at all, and not a Porta-Potty in sight.

Rating ★★★★☆

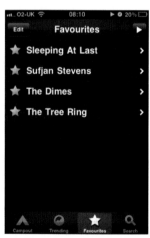

■ Your Favourites list is a great resource that allows you to return to bands you like

■ The random selection provided by the app is a great way to discover bands you might otherwise miss

Price: £9.99/$15.99   Developer: Augmentra Ltd

ViewRanger Outdoors GPS (Premium)

A comprehensive and good-value outdoor mapping solution

Outdoor mapping is a feature that is offered in many apps, but very few manage to bring a solution that is worth using on every trip. Some try to cover the whole of the UK in basic detail and others cost a lot of money to provide comprehensive info. The premium version of ViewRanger Outdoors GPS does neither and lets you choose the maps and locations you require from the premium credit that is built in to the app. You can choose to install all UK national parks and two specific regions, and then further enhance the map sets by using the unlimited access to street map layers for the UK, which is ideal for cyclists or general sightseeing.

Despite the fact that most who use this kind of app will not require many extra features, they are included. Trails are available including photos and extra information, and the visual guidance will ensure that you are never off track. You can share your location with others in your party, which is an excellent safety feature, and you can also record and save each track. This is particularly useful because you may know better routes than any app can offer, and you can then share these with others as you please.

The interface and presentation fits the genre perfectly and takes the value of this app to a new level. When compared to dedicated hardware solutions for outdoor mapping, this makes the app feel incredibly cheap. This may well lead some to believe that it could never compete, but it truly does and offers a solution that will work for the majority of people who require an app like this. We'd love to list all of the features and gush over how well they work, but alas we cannot. We are able, however, to conclude that this is a near-perfect outdoor mapping solution for anyone who owns an iPhone.

Rating ★★★★★

■ Even the overview maps offer a sense of perspective

■ The level of detail is incredibly high

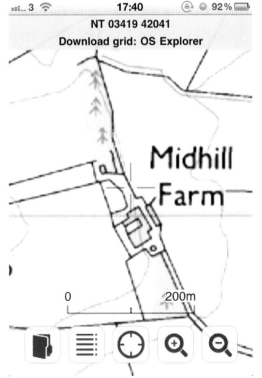

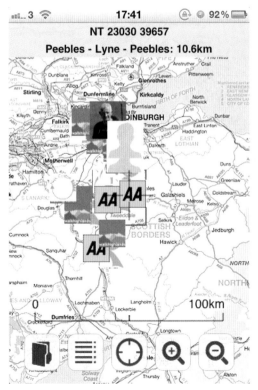

■ Every video you record is stored until you've reviewed or deleted it

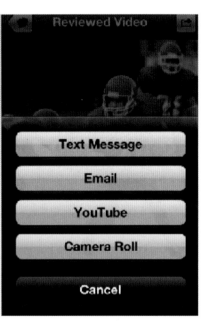

■ Reviewed videos can be shared via several outlets, including social networks and sites like YouTube

■ Once you've analysed your video, it can be saved to the Reviewed section where you can go back to it at any point

Price: £2.99/$4.99 **Developer:** TechSmith Corporation

Coach's Eye
Become the sporting pundit you've always wanted to be

There are plenty of dads out there who coach their kids' sports teams, and maybe take it a bit too seriously. Well, now there is an app to take their obsession to the next level. Coach's Eye is a video app that allows you to get analytical with what you record – for example, your son's football game – and point out the key plays. The app comes with screen-drawing abilities similar to those you see on TV coverage of most sports these days, but scaled down so you can take it with you on your iPhone, for personal use.

The controls for editing and analysing what you've captured are very straightforward, with a scrolling button that allows you to move through the footage in slow-motion, which potentially makes this app suitable for use in presentations. There is a slow-motion button you can use if you don't want to manually slow down the footage, making this advanced feature very easy to use. You can then draw and highlight different things within your video – for example, a player out of position or a run about

to be made by a player – using the wheel menu, which allows you to draw freehand or place arrows, boxes or other shapes within your footage.

Once you've finished your analysis, you can save your videos to the Reviewed section of the app and go back to them at any time, as well as share them through social media sites like Twitter and Facebook, or via email.

The only real drawback with the app is that you can't upload pre-recorded videos into Coach's Eye, which does mean a fair amount of planning ahead is needed when you want to analyse your team's plays. Of course, it also means having your iPhone at the ready at all times, as opposed to filming on another camera and then importing it into this app later. This is a shame, as it does feel like a restriction that could limit usage slightly, but nonetheless there will still be those obsessive coaches who will go over their team's work with Coach's Eye.

Rating

Korg iKaossillator

Create inspired musical chaos with Korg iKaossillator

Price: £13.99/$19.99 Developer: KORG INC.

■ Changing the lengths of loops can create some unique results

■ There are plenty of pre-loaded phrases that cover a variety of styles

Having previously focused on the iPad, Korg's latest offering, the Korg iKoassilator, allows both iPhone and iPad users to get in on the action.

Based upon the popular Kaoss controller series of music tools, the iKaossilator is an expressive musical implement that caters for both musicians and non-musicians alike.

The main interface focuses on a musical loop consisting of five parts. Using the interface, musical phrases can be swapped with one of the many that come with the app. Alternatively, individual sounds can be chosen and played via the touchscreen interface. Any completed masterpieces can be exported to SoundCloud, AudioCopied to other apps or simply saved as a .WAV for use in desktop studio applications. The included sounds are up to the excellent Korg standard, and with a little work some solid loops can be swiftly created. Within the small space of an iPhone display, Korg have managed to provide a fun yet powerful musical tool.

Rating ★★★★★

Mozy

Back up to the Cloud, and access your files anywhere

Price: Free Developer: Decho Corporation

Mozy gives you the chance to take your computer with you wherever you go. It gives you access to all of your backed-up files that have been stored in the Cloud via Mozy's desktop client.

The interface may be basic, but the layout mimics your desktop, making a search for your folders easy. You get security via Mozy's encryptions, but you can also create a passcode.

The app's best feature is its speed. Images load quickly and in high quality. Plus, you can share files via social networks and email.

The fact that you can read all your documents using the app's built-in reader is also a massive plus, especially as this has been a letdown in some Cloud-supporting apps.

These features make Mozy ideal for meetings and commutes, as you always feel close to your desktop hub and are never caught out by an awkward question in a meeting, especially knowing the answer is on your computer.

Rating ★★★★☆

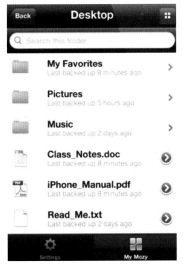

■ Images load quickly and in high quality, and you can share files via social networks and email

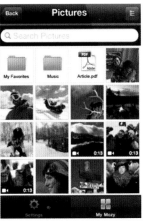

■ The app uses the layout of your desktop to organise files

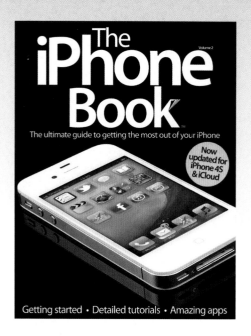

Learn in style

The Book Series

Discover more with the Book series' expert, accessible tutorials for iPad, iPhone, Mac, Android, Photoshop, Windows and more